the
NEW
FOREST

One of the many sites you will be greeted by as you explore the New Forest.

the
NEW
FOREST

Mathew Conway

The
History
Press

First published 2010

The History Press
The Mill, Brimscombe Port
Stroud, Gloucestershire, GL5 2QG
www.thehistorypress.co.uk

Reprinted 2015

British Library Cataloguing in Publication Data.
A catalogue record for this book is available from the British Library.

ISBN 978 0 7524 4932 6

Typesetting and origination by The History Press
Printed in Great Britain

CONTENTS

INTRODUCTION

The New Forest will always have a special place in my heart – although I was born in London (I always say London even though others may say Essex) my family and I moved down to the South Coast not long after I hit double figures. We started off in Poole and soon made our way over to Bournemouth. During my early teens at Poole Grammar School the Forest was little more than a pretty collection of trees that I would pass through on the train on my not so frequent jaunts to London. However, when my education took me to a sixth-form college in the heart of Brockenhurst my intimate relationship with the Forest began. Every moment you spent at the college you knew you were in the Forest. Just outside the main entrance there was a small plot of land covered with Shetland Ponies and I would often spot rabbits, hares and deer through the trees. At lunch time, or during the odd lesson that I skipped (I was not always the perfect student) my friends and I would go for a walk down into Brockenhurst and enjoy the feel of the small town with its many little local shops.

For many reasons the two years that I spent at Brockenhurst College were by far the best of my life. There is a good chance that I am romanticising the past, but I do not have the same feelings about university or for any other period of my life before or since. I made some good friends that I still have and it is there that I fell in love with nature and wildlife.

Most of my time at the college and the town itself was idyllic – but there was one event that will always stay in my mind. Foot and Mouth disease.

Living in Bournemouth, I was amongst people that were generally isolated from the horrors of the crisis. It was true that I saw stories on the news about it but it was all so far removed. But I remember clearly how on one day I went to college and suddenly all the animals that I was so used to seeing had suddenly disappeared, all the gates were shut and disinfectant mats had been placed everywhere. My normal city existence no longer sheltered me from the reality of the disease. It was sad for me to see the animals disappearing; I can only begin to imagine what it must have been like for all the farmers who lost livestock, for all the people whose lives depended on their animals.

It was a dark day for Brockenhurst and the New Forest, but it is one that the wonderful place has recovered from. The mats are no longer there and wildlife and history abounds in every square inch of the National Park. During the course of this book I will take you to some of the places that are dearest to me, I will tell you the most interesting stories about the New Forest and I will, of course, introduce you to the wonderful wildlife that it has to offer.

Mathew Conway, 2010

HOW TO USE THIS BOOK

At one point England was covered in trees, but as civilisation dawned the great forests dwindled, being replaced first by farms and villages and then by the towns, cities and airports of today. The New Forest is often described as one of the last of the great forests of England. Without doubt it is one of the largest areas of undeveloped and unenclosed land in the south of Britain, an area that is enjoyed by millions of visitors each year.

It has gone through many changes from its creation in 1079 to its designation as a National Park in 2005. It was used as a filming location for the film *Robin Hood Prince of Thieves* and was the setting for the death of two members of royalty. It has supplied timber for the navy and it has been a training ground for our troops during two world wars and, of course, it is home to countless animals. Whatever you are after you can probably find it within the 92,000 acres that the New Forest covers.

This book is as eclectic as the Forest itself, falling somewhere between a history book and a guidebook, hopefully with some nice photographs to look at along the way. Some history, tales of interest and folklore will adorn the pages, all the while with the focus being around wildlife. Throughout the book there will be tips on where to best see the animals mentioned as well as some general guidance on how to approach them.

The book is written and split up in such a way that you can dip in and out, or read it in order – but remember, this is a book about the New Forest, and the best way to get a feel for it, and to experience the National Park, is to get out there yourself. Towards the end of

the book there is a chapter summarising some of the different places that you can visit in the Forest, how best to get there and explore and even a section on how best to take some photographs!

One last thing before you continue, if you are going to be hiking through the Forest please take a moment to read the brief section about doing it responsibly, the Forest has been around for thousands of years, and it would be nice if it was around for thousands more to come.

The Forest has been around for thousands of years; some areas have remained virtually unchanged, whereas other areas will be unrecognisable.

one

THE HISTORY OF THE NEW FOREST

From the Iron Age through to you reading this book the New Forest has changed a great deal; it has seen invaders and wars, great storms and extinctions, witches and snake catchers, gypsies and royalty. History has left its mark on the Forest just as the Forest itself has left its mark on history.

This section deals with the history of the forest, from its creation as a Royal Forest to its evolution into a National Park. It is by no means a comprehensive history, but the major points are covered and throughout the section you will see hints and tips on how you can get a little closer to the history, interact with the forest, and, if you are lucky, feel it come to life.

🌺 THE BIRTH OF THE NEW FOREST 🌺

You would have thought one battle would have been enough, with one invader dismissed just weeks ago another had reared its head and all because the King had died. Arrows flew through the sky from the Norman archers, arcing high up and almost disappearing from sight until suddenly turning and slamming down towards them. But their wall of shields was holding. The Normans would not be breaking them any time soon, and to hell with them all if they thought William, Duke of Normandy, would be the new King of England. Still … he was tired, they were all tired, they had rushed here from the battle at Stamford Bridge, picking up whatever new men they could on the way. But Harold had something to prove, he wanted to show everyone that he was the rightful heir of Edward the Confessor, that he could defend the borders from any invader, that he was King of England.

Another hail of arrows rained down, but his shield held firm. The enemy's archers were not having the affect they wanted; the English ranks were not being thinned. But then they charged. He could see the infantry storming up the hill with nothing but kill or be killed on their minds. Those around him with javelins fired upon the onrushing masses, but he had no such weapon. What he and others did have were stones, and they rained death upon the Normans. He smiled, many of them were falling. This was going to be a day for the English.

The Bayeux Tapestry, depicting Harold's death.

> *But even though their colleagues were falling around them the Normans kept coming. As they drew closer they gained individuality, you could make out their faces, soon you would be able to see their eyes. And everyone knew what happened when you could see the white of their eyes …*
>
> *He drew his sword, now the real fight would begin.*

As with anything, it is usually a good idea to start with the name. For this we need to look back to William the Conqueror and 1066, a name and date that everyone knows from their schooldays. The country had just lost one King, Edward the Confessor, who had died in January of that year. As is so often the case when a monarch dies, a power vacuum ensued, with a resultant struggle over succession to the throne. In the wake of his death there were three main contenders for the crown: Harold, who held the kingship for nine months, Harald Hardrada the King of Norway, and the then William, Duke of Normandy – after his successful invasion of England better known as William the Conqueror.

Hardrada made his attempt to seize the country and claim kingship by coming over in September with an invasion force, but he was defeated on 25 September 1066 at Stamford Bridge, just outside York, by the armies of Harold. However, while this had been happening the much delayed armies of William and his allies

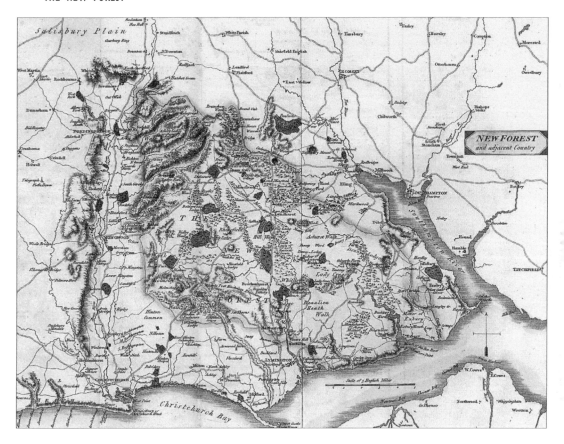

A map of the New Forest, c. 1800.

had finally managed to cross the English Channel. They landed unopposed at Peversey on 28 September. Despite the English troops being tired from battle, and a warning from one of his brothers that they should delay and assemble more men, Harold decided to rush down to meet the invading William in what he considered a show of strength. But on 14 October, just sixteen days later, Harold was defeated and famously killed with an arrow through the eye. William was King of the English. Thirteen years later, in 1079, the New Forest, a Royal Forest, was created.

It is important to understand the use of the word 'forest' – it differs from the everyday English usage, where it simply refers to a large, dense collection of trees. When one is talking about the New Forest, it has a very specific meaning; in fact, it even has a legal definition: it was an area of land, reserved for hunting and the term 'forest' was given by Royal Prerogative to an area of land in which Forest Law applied. This is why the boundary of the New Forest is not simply where the tree-line stops, it includes heather, marsh, coastline and a variety of different habitats. It is all part of the beauty

An extract from the Domesday Book showing the New Forest's first official mention as the Nova Foresta.

of the New Forest; it supports numerous other environments leading to the rich and diverse wildlife, that if you take the time, you can find and enjoy.

The process of creating the New Forest was called afforestation. This does not, as one would expect, mean the opposite of deforestation, the removal of trees. Instead, it is the legal creation of the forest and the application of Forest Law. In the case of the New Forest, this involved the razing of over twenty villages and the removal of many of the people who lived there. This was just

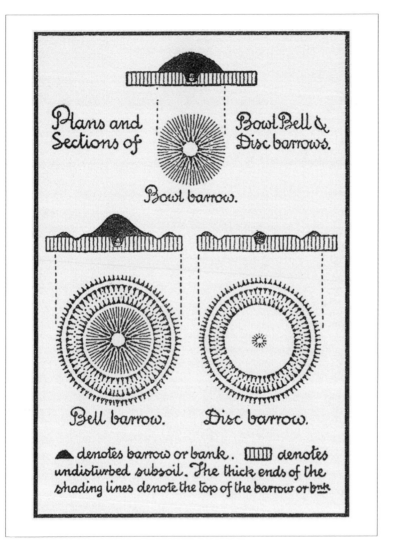

Some of the different types of barrow you can spot around the New Forest.

the start of what was going to be an unhappy relationship between the inhabitants of the Forest and the monarchy, something that was going to be made worse by the harsh application of Forest Law.

And so it was that, by royal decree, the New Forest was created – the first instance of its name being recorded was in the Domesday Book, in 1086, as the 'Nova Foresta'.

Even though the term Forest has a very specific meaning here it does not take away the fact that the area is, indeed, largely wooded and the area had, of course, existed long before its designation and definition by William the Conqueror.

Today there is little of the woodland left that used to cover the UK as the process of deforestation started thousands of years ago with the first instance of civilisation on our shores. The reason for the existence of such a large amount of woodland in the New Forest is a simple one: the soil. It is of surprisingly poor quality, little can be grown on it and it is therefore of little use for cultivation. This has meant that very little was ever cleared for use. Another advantage of this is that, while development in other areas of the country destroyed archaeological clues, many sites in the New Forest have been left relatively untouched, preserving traces of ancient agriculture, industry and civilisation. There are over some 250 round barrows as well as over 150 scheduled monuments within the Forest boundaries. Most of the barrows are located around the village of Beaulieu. Unfortunately, over time many have been damaged by vandalism or by looters, undoubtedly looking for treasure, but there is very little contained in them of monetary worth.

During the Iron Age small amounts of land were cleared as technology improved. One of the small hilltop forts that were built during this era can be seen on Castle Hill at Burley, whilst there are a few others dotted around the Forest.

The Romans cultivated a little more land, kept livestock and even set up a thriving pottery industry here in AD 300, as evidenced by the remains of a large Roman villa at Rockbourne. It is also believed that a Roman road ran from Nursling to Stoney Cross, but the best preserved sections were destroyed by the creation of the M27 in 1974.

Some of the different archaeological finds, as well as a graphical tour of the New Forest's history, can be found at the New Forest Museum in Lyndhurst (*see* 'Places to Visit' for more information).

But even as different societies tried to live in and cultivate the Forest the problem of poor soil quality did not go away, and many of the trees remained. Life continued, people lived in and around the area, but up until William the Conqueror in 1066, it was merely a collection of trees, not a Forest.

🌸 HUNTING 🌸

Dawn was his favourite time of day, the light was new and fresh, and the deer were stirring, foraging around, it was by far the best time to find them. He bent over as he spotted a deer track. A fully grown adult judging by the size of it, a few more moments searching revealed some droppings. Fresh. It was going to be a good day for a hunt. Still, he thought, he had to locate it, see it with his own eyes, before heading back to camp. He was the expert huntsmen, returning empty handed, without the information they needed, was not an option.

His dog tugged at the leash; it had picked up the scent, but the well-trained animal contained its excitement, not even letting out the smallest of yelps, merely indicating the direction they needed to go. Quietly stalking the prey they moved off, looking for the most noble of creatures, the hart, the male red deer.

Ten more minutes of silently moving through the Forest and they were upon it, a proud and noble creature, the only one truly worthy of the hunt. With the quarry found it was time to return, the hunt would begin this afternoon. As he walked off shame filled him from the boots up, in his excitement he had let his concentration wander, and his foot crumpled a twig underneath as he placed his weight upon it; as good a warning to the deer as a near miss with an arrow. The animal turned, looking for a moment at the source of the disturbance before darting off between the trees.

It was not all bad news though, he knew where the deer had been, and the direction it was going in – he was pretty sure he knew where it would end up. It was time to head back, to enjoy the feast of break-fast and to plan the day's hunt.

For much of its history the main purpose of the New Forest was as a hunting ground. Hunting had always been important to all levels of society, both as a source of food and as pest control, but for the Normans it was something much more. It was a pastime, something for the aristocracy to do, both socially and as training for war – during a hunt one would have to practice all the skills that were necessary in battle.

William the Conqueror was no different; indeed he was hunting in Rouen when he heard the news of Harold taking the throne. It is for this reason that William the Conqueror created the New Forest in 1079, as a place to indulge his love of hunting as well as to supply the Royal household with meat. Interestingly enough, the Normans' obsession with hunting left its mark on the English language. Unlike most other languages, we have two separate words for the animal and the meat. Pig is pork, from the French *porc*, if you were eating sheep it would be called mutton, from the French *mouton*, then there is cow and beef, from the French *boeuf* (although this originally referred to oxen) and deer, for which we know the meat as venison, coming from the French *la venison* literally meaning 'the game we just hunted'.

It was not just the name of the food that was in French, the whole of the terminology of the hunt, which in itself was vast, was in the same tongue. This terminology would be a perquisite for anyone wanting to be a knight; indeed, learning it all was part of the training. From the Norman invasion onwards hunting was an integral part of aristocratic life, making its way into folklore and literature.

As previously mentioned, hunting was in many ways similar to war in terms of the skills needed, and was often seen as a form of preparation. Going out on any hunt involved the use of the same weapons as would be used in combat; the bow and arrow, swords and spears. Much later it would also involve the use of the crossbow and eventually the gun – though both of these weapons changed the nature of the hunt and how huntsmen were perceived. Women would sometimes accompany the hunt, using cudgels to kill any small game that they encountered on the way. The hunt itself was, in many ways, similar to the modern fox hunt, with a strong emphasis on the horse and the hound, but there was also the addition of hawks (a generic term referring to both hawks and falcons).

The horse

One of the most famous residents of the New Forest is of course its pony. The New Forest Pony can be spotted on even the briefest of walks through the Forest – but these are far removed from the type of animal that would have been used in hunting. Horses were a

You can still see many ponies and horses being ridden through the New Forest.

fundamental part of the nobleman's household, with different horses serving different purposes, just as they do today. There would be pack and carthorses for day-to-day work and menial tasks, palfreys for normal riding and destriers or coursers for war. These are not necessarily different breeds; the difference between a palfrey and a destrier may simply be one of speed and strength. The names were a classification of what they were capable of doing and the use that they were put to, not of breed. An all-purpose horse was known as a rouncer, and this too was occasionally used during times of war. Those used in hunting were generally the courser or a well-bred palfrey, either way the horse would need strength and stamina to be able to keep up with the quarry over long distances and to be able to deal with the uneven, ever changing terrain.

The hound

Dogs played an important part throughout the duration of the hunt. Dogs were, of course, essential in finding and tracking prey, but they were also used to distract, drive or even kill the quarry. Due to the wide range of tasks undertaken, different dogs were used during different parts of the hunt – a small dog with a good sense of smell would be no use when the animal was at bay, a spaniel could hardly face down a wild boar.

An example of this specialised use was the greyhound, a fast dog that was able to take down game but with poor stamina and so unable to chase the quarry over long distances. They would therefore ride with the hunter and only be released before the close of the hunt, when the animal was both in sight and where the hunters wanted it to be. The alaunt, a now extinct breed, or the mastiff, would be used against larger, more dangerous prey such as boars.

Before the animal could be faced down ready for the kill, you had the chase, and for this you needed fast dogs, with good stamina, while still having a decent sense of smell – the breed of dogs used, runninghounds (similar to today's foxhounds), were known as rache. For tracking a sense of smell was paramount and a lymer (a dog on a leash), such as a bloodhound, would be used. In a typical hunting group there would be a couple of lymers and around twenty rache.

As with the horses, dogs were an important part of the household and would be treated with due reverence. They lived in kennels on oak beds, with a page usually sleeping with them, to stop them fighting and to care for the sick. Their houses would be on two floors, allowing the dogs to escape the ground floor if it was either too hot or too cold – all in all they were treated extremely well.

A kestrel hunting.

The hawk

Falconry was, and still is, an art, with training being long and often dangerous. After the bird had been selected, usually a female both for her size and her slightly better disposition towards cooperation, they would seel her. The process of seeling would involve the eyes being sewn shut, in a similar way that hawks are hooded today – to stop them being scared of distracted. The trainer would carry her on their arm until the bird was used to it, the eyes would then gradually be unsewn and training prey, such as herons with broken legs, would be introduced to finalise its skills for the hunt.

Hawks of the tower, in medieval terminology referred to falcons, with hawks of the fist being hawks as we think of them. Commonly used birds at the time were goshawks and sparrowhawks, the peregrine, gyrfalcon, merlin and hobby falcons, many of which can still be seen wild in the Forest. To get a closer glimpse into the practice of falconry you can take some short courses in the Forest (*see* 'Places to Visit').

The day

There were two main ways in which the hunt was undertaken, the first, by bow and stable, was the simplest and often the most effective. An entire herd would be rounded up by dogs and driven to a predetermined location where archers would be laying in wait, killing the herd on mass.

The second method, by far considered the more noble of the two, was *par force de chiens*, by force of dogs. This type of hunt would last the entire day and was divided into eight parts:

Quest – Before the hunt could begin the hunters would need to find their prey. For this bit a sole huntsmen, an expert at finding and tracking animals, would head off. With him he would take a lymer (a dog on the leash with a strong sense of smell) until he found traces of a deer. He would be looking for the same signs that you would if you went to the Forest today – tracks, sounds, and of course droppings. Their task would be to find the location of the deer as accurately as possible and report back.

Assembly – As the name suggests, all those going on the hunt would gather. It would be the social start of the day and a breakfast would be served. Before the next phase of the hunt, they would plan the day, discussing what the huntsmen had discovered during the quest.

Relays – Still more preparation would occur as sets of dogs were placed along the predicted path of the deer. This means that there would be fresh dogs available as the hunt progressed, ensuring that the deer would always be under the pressure of the chase.

Moving – This is the last part before the chase, and it involved pinning down the exact location of the deer. A lymer was used to find it and the hunt would then begin.

Chase – This is when the real hunt, as we think of it, began – the deer would run and the dogs and hunters would give chase. This is when good dogs and a good horse would pay off, ones with the stamina, strength and agility to deal with the uneven terrain.

Baying – This occurred when the animal was at bay – after a long chase the deer would eventually run out of energy, being unable to run any further. It would not just give in though, like any animal backed into a corner it would turn and fight. While the dogs were stopped from attacking, but still used to distract the quarry, the lead huntsmen would approach and kill the animal, usually with a sword or spear.

Unmaking – The now dead animal would be cut apart in a ritualistic manner.

Curée – Lastly the dogs would be rewarded for their efforts with meat from the animal, helping to reinforce their training.

The modern-day hunt

The hunt was not simply something that only existed in William the Conqueror's time; it evolved and changed as social fashions did. The modern hunting era in the New Forest started with the creation of the New Forest Hounds in 1781. They were involved in four types of hunting. Originally, the then Master of the Hunt favoured black dogs, hence the name blackhounds, whilst there were also the foxhounds, the otterhounds and the beagles (for chasing hares). However, with the passing of the Hunting Act of 2004 hunting became illegal from 18 February 2005.

Hunts still continue today but in a much altered form. Instead of chasing live animals an artificial trail is used. A scent is laid and the dogs follow it. Often road kill is used and hunting is seen as an efficient way of dealing with the problem.

The modern hunt still bears some similarities to its predecessor – instead of the assembly there is the meet, which is at 10.45 a.m. and lasts for around half an hour, this is largely a social part of the day and a small drink is often enjoyed. After this the huntsman sounds his horn and moves off with the hounds who will search for the scent. The hunt will begin as soon as the scent is found with the day ending at around three or four o'clock in the afternoon.

❧ THE QUARRY ❧

Proud and tall the stag stood there, occasionally bending its slender neck to pick up and consume a well-suited acorn – the creature paused and turned, sunlight glancing off his tree like antlers. He breathed in, succulent forest air filled his nostrils. Something was there and whatever or whoever it was, its scent had betrayed its presence. He looked around, carefully, slowly, not dashing off yet. They may not have spotted him; the commotion of darting off may well give him away. A rustle of leaves, the scent of dogs in the air, they were getting closer. And there were a lot of them.

Powerful muscles in his legs tensed, coiling up energy, ready to spring him off at a moment's notice – behind him, they were there, now he was sure, he could hear them coming, he could hear the hunt, he could hear the hunters. His legs released as his hooves dug into the ground, pushing him forward. Ceaseless energy flowed through his body, bounding, darting between the trees. But the dogs had him now,

> *they had his scent, they were not going to let him go. What they did not know was the path he would take. This was his forest, not theirs. He galloped on, every muscle in his body, every fibre of his being knowing it was a chase he needed to win, there was no second place.*
>
> *The scents changed, new dogs joined in as the old ones tired out … there was no getting away. He stumbled, almost falling over. His energy waned, his speed dropped. This was it. If he had not lost them by now he wasn't going to. They had not been lost at all, they were right behind him.*
>
> *He stopped and turned to face the dogs. No more running. Time to fight.*

The quarry of the hunt usually consisted of three animals: deer, which are still abundant and varied within the forest; Wild Boar, now returned to places in the UK but not (at the time of writing) in the Forest; and the wolf, now extinct within the UK – the only animal on the list to have been deliberately hunted to extinction. One creature, for which you can find detailed hunting instructions in medieval literature, that has never, or at least credibly, been spotted, is the unicorn. The instructions are clear – you must get the beast to lie down on the lap of a virgin where it would then be docile enough to snare. There are even warnings against trying to trick the mythical creature into charging a tree and getting its horn stuck.

Deer – Of all the animals that one could hunt during the Middle Ages, it was the deer that was the most prized. The fallow, roe and red deer accounted for three of the five royal beasts of the chase and the deer's existence was the very reason for the creation of the Forest. The deer had much symbolic significance for the Normans, with some equating its suffering during the hunt to that of Christ. Some legends even talk of a bone at the centre of a deer's heart that stopped it dying of fear.

In the modern–day New Forest you can find five different species of deer, but only two of which are native to the British Isles. These two are the roe (*Caprelous capreolus*) and red deer (*Cervus elaphus*).

Just to be confusing, the male, female and the young of each species of deer are referred to slightly differently, below is a list of which deer is called what as well as other terms that you might hear an experienced deer watcher use.

Species	Male	Female	Young
Red	Stag/Hart	Hind	Calf
Sika	Stag	Hind	Calf
Fallow	Buck	Doe	Fawn
Muntjac	Buck	Doe	Fawn
Roe	Buck	Doe	Kid

Term	Definition
Pelage	The coat
Slots	Track marks
Fewments	Deer droppings
Tine	Point on an antler
Rut	The mating season
Small Deer	A herd of female fallow deer
Pearling	Raised bumps on the antlers of a roe deer
Coronet	Base of antler
Pedicle	The raised section on the skull from which the antlers grow
Speller	Points on a fallow deer's antler
Palmation	The shape of a fallow deer's antlers
Brocket	Yearling Red/Sika stag

Red deer, the biggest of all the five species, and one of the biggest you can get anywhere in the world, are kept at a roughly constant level of 100 within the boundaries of the New Forest. Their colouring changes with the season, with a rich chestnut pelage (see above for an explanation of terminology) in the summer, and grey-brown in winter. In medieval times the male of the species was known as a hart, whereas now they are more often referred to as a stag (see the table above for the naming conventions of the different deer). The male can be up to 230cm long and 190kg in weight and they have bone antlers for around six months of the year – each year they are shed, and grow again from scratch at a staggering 2.5cm a day. During spring the newly formed antlers will have a soft fur covering to help protect them.

Members of a herd of red deer roaming around the New Forest.

It was the male red deer that was the most prized animal for hunting. The so called Hart of Ten was the utmost trophy – a Hart of Ten is a male red deer with ten tines (ten points on its antlers).

The best place to spot red deer is at the deer park in front of the Burley Manor Hotel. You will not be guaranteed a sighting, but if you are short of time it is your best bet. Another good place is Ober Heath, near Brockenhurst, though they tend to be on the far side. Remember dawn and dusk are the best time for spotting red deer.

Roe deer are the other species that are native to the British Isles and there are about 350 of them to be found roaming amongst the trees of the New Forest. Unlike red deer, they tend to be more solitary, not moving in herds, though sometimes they can be spotted in pairs or within family groups. They rut in July, far earlier than the other species, but give birth at the same time of year – this is down to the fact that the embryo does not attach to the womb until a few months after fertilisation. Their name, roe, comes from the old English *ro*, meaning streaked of spotted. Roe deer are unusual in the fact that they regrow their antlers as soon as they are shed, with no prolonged delay like with other types of deer. They are far smaller than red deer, at about 60–70kg for the males, and shoulders at a height of about 70cm. With a uniform coat of ginger-red in the summer and a grey-brown in winter and a white marking just above their top lip they are easy to identify if you can find them.

Roe deer are particularly hard to spot as they are small and will disappear deep into the forest when they see, or more likely hear, you. Open areas on the edge of the forest are often a good place to see them, although you will need a good dose of luck. Again dusk and dawn are the best times of day to try and get a sighting.

The remaining three species have been introduced to the British Isles over the last few thousand years with varying success. The first of the new species to be introduced was the fallow deer (*Dama dama*) – another popular one for the hunt.

For a long time it was believed that the Normans brought the deer to the country. However, recent evidence from Fishbourne Palace has found the remains of fallow deer dating from the first century AD. Some of these deer may have escaped to establish a colony. However, it seems likely that the Normans were responsible for their widespread establishment.

They are of average size, around 90kg in weight and with a shoulder height of around 1m, making them larger than the native roe, but smaller than red deer. The New Forest is home to around 2,000 of the creatures and it is considered one of the most wild herds in the country. However, the herd does include some recent park escapes and these have introduced new colours into the area. You can now, if you are lucky, spot the following: white (creamy off-white, not albino), menil (brightly spotted), melanistic (very dark brown) and common (spotted in the summer, dull grey-brown in the winter). Unlike red deer, their antlers are flat and large, not tree like.

If you come across a fallow deer and disturb it, keep an eye out, it may well just run to nearby cover instead of disappearing completely. A place for an almost guaranteed sighting is at

The very distinctive fallow deer.

Bolderwood, near Lymington. They leave out food for the deer at around two o'clock in the afternoon and you will often see the deer grazing in the sun. On the same road (heading back towards the A35) you can stop off to see the Knightwood Oak (*see* 'Tales of Trees and Other Plants'). There is another enclosure not far from Brockenhurst, adjacent to the cycle path to Lyndhurst (*see* 'A Few Walks' for precise instructions on how to reach it).

The last two types of deer are sika (*Cervus nippon*) and muntjac (*Muntiacus reevesi*). Sika are a Japanese species of deer that first escaped from a herd owned by Lord Montagu in Beaulieu in 1902. Originally a single pair escaped, but Lord Montagu later released a second breeding pair to keep them company. Unusually for the UK, the New Forest stock is considered to be clean, with no interbreeding having occurred. Interbreeding, though, is considered a potential problem by the Forestry Commission. If they cross breed with red deer the offspring is fertile, thereby threatening the purity of one of our native species – it is for this reason that they area accepted within one area, but not the entire Forest. The best place to spot them is around Brockenhurst, especially near more boggy areas.

While a similar size to roe deer, they have dark stripe alone their spine and a white rump. Antlers are branched with four points.

The Muntjac is the most distinctive sounding of all the deer in the Forest, giving off a loud barking noise, which is why it also known as the barking deer. If taken by surprise you may well think you heard a dog. From China originally, the UK stock escaped from Woburn Park in the late nineteenth century. Within the New Forest there is a no-tolerance policy due to the competition they pose to roe deer – part of the problem is that they breed all year, with no specific mating season like the others. Not that common and easily scared, they can be hard to spot, but you will know them when you hear one.

If you are extremely lucky then you may be fortunate enough to lay your eyes on a genetic oddity. Red deer, instead of having their usual brown hue, can, on occasion, be white. This is not down to any albino traits, instead it is caused by a genetic mutation that is held in a recessive gene – that is to say it must inherit it from both its the mother and father must both have it for the offspring to be born white, otherwise it will be brown like its parents.

The white hart, as it is known, is part of legends both old and new. It is said that it appeared to King Arthur as a signal to embark on a quest. In France if you kill one a curse of unrequited love would be laid upon you. Today, if you see one, then not only are you lucky for spotting it, but you should be rewarded far more luck in return. They are so rare that only a handful are thought to exist in Britain.

A white hart was spotted in 2008 in the Forest, so seeing one is not beyond possibility, it is even believed that this one may be a direct descendent from the one that was caught be Henry VII in the fifteenth century. Upon capturing the beast, as the story goes, he marched it to Ringwood where he displayed it, and this is where the area's first pub bearing the name the White Hart was erected. Today the White Hart is the fifth most popular pub name in Britain.

The locations of white harts are normally kept a secret for the simple reason that their rarity means they fetch a large price on the black market – their stuffed heads reaching several thousand pounds in value. Rather sadly in 2007 a white hart on the border between Devon and Cornwall was found hung in a tree, its head removed to sell on to a collector … who knows what curse befell them.

The boar – During the period when wild boar were common in the New Forest they were considered a difficult beast to hunt, one which required much bravery and skill. They could be much more ferocious than deer, especially when backed into a corner. It was not unknown for them to kill dogs, horses and even the men that were hunting them. It was for this very reason that hunting wild boar was

One of the many wild boar that are in captivity around the country.

seen as such a good way for honing one's skills for the battlefield. If facing a boar was not considered dangerous enough, some would increase the challenge, and the risk, by waiting until mating season; during this time the males would be even more aggressive than normal and far more likely to attack anyone who approached them.

As with deer, the boar would be hunted *par force de chiens* but here it was more important for the dogs not to attack, as there was a good chance that the well-bred, expensive canine would not win the fight. The kill would be done by a rider with a spear, or more traditionally a noble would dismount and finish it with a dagger, though for this you needed more than just a little bit of bravery, or to be a tad foolhardy.

During the Middle Ages the boar became extinct within the British Isles, but farming of the creature began during the 1980s, and, as with all of these things, creatures escaped over the decades and during the 1990s the boar managed to re-establish itself in certain areas. One such population is in Dorset, with some sources saying they have been making their way towards the New Forest. If you would like to see wild boar then you can always take a visit to the New Forest Wildlife Park (formerly the New Forest Otter, Owl and Wildlife Park). Here they have numerous animals, including boar (*see* 'Places to Visit').

The wolf – The wolf has always been an animal that has inspired fear and wonder in people, regardless of where the live, both as a threat to livestock and a few unfortunate people. So much so that they have made their way into numerous rhymes and fairy tales – we all know the stories of the girl in a red riding hood and the one of the pigs in their variously constructed houses. Because of the threat they posed they were the only one of the five royal beasts of the chase that a commoner could hunt – outside of the Royal Forests of course. During the Norman era servants were employed to hunt wolves, being granted lands in return. Edward I (1272-1307) ordered their extinction but it was not until Henry VII's reign (1485-1509) that the last one was killed and they no longer graced our shores. If you want to see a wild wolf you will not have any luck in the British Isles. The wolf was not eaten like the deer or the boar but its pelt was sometimes used for cloaks or gloves if one was willing to put up with the smell they inevitably carried. Again, if you would like to see one while in the New Forest you can always pay a visit to the New Forest Wildlife Park where they have recently acquired several wolves.

Other prey – Some other animals were hunted purely for the sport of it: the fox, the otter and the badger are some of the creatures that you can find in the New Forest. They were considered inedible and so hunted for the thrill of the chase alone. One other animal that could be hunted both for fun and for its meat was the hare – greyhounds would chase down the animals by sight alone, in what is known as coursing. Over the centuries this developed into modern-day greyhound racing.

❀ THE COMMONERS, THEIR ANIMALS ❀ AND FOREST LAW

What on earth had gone through his mind? What thought process had led him to that decision? Well, that much had been easy: his children. They were hungry. Actually to hell with his kids, he was hungry. And it had been so tempting, standing there, just ... standing. It hadn't been doing anything, it hadn't run, hadn't hidden. The creature had just emerged from the edge of the wood and carried on into his land. It wasn't even a particularly impressive deer. It was just a deer. Enough food to feed him and his family for a week.

He knew you weren't supposed to. He knew what would happen to you if you tried. The deer were off limits. The deer were not to be touched. The deer belonged to the King.

That had been two days ago, he had been caught and tried. Now he was being punished.

'Place your hands on the log,' commanded a voice from above him.

At least he had missed the deer. He wasn't going to die.

'Put your hands on the log,' the voice didn't sound like it would ask a third time.

Hesitantly he raised his arms, placing his hands, palm down, on the oak log that they had placed in front of him.

He closed his eyes and took a deep breath in. The axe swung down ...

Damn the King and his forest laws.

As much as William the Conqueror would have liked the New Forest to be nothing more than his private hunting ground, people had lived there long before the Normans arrived and they have continued to do so right through until this day. It is from these two groups having to co-exist that both the Forest Laws and Commoner's rights have arisen and evolved.

Forest laws

Just as the Forest was created, so the laws were created and enacted by William the Conqueror with the aim of preserving the game that he so loved to hunt. The laws, their implementation and the treatment of those who violated them, caused a great deal of resentment amongst the residents of the Forest – it was part of the reason that he was so hated by those who dwelt in the Forest, something evidenced by a poem written on his death. The 'Rime of King William' featured in the Peterborough Chronicle in 1087, the year of William's death. Part of the modern translation is given below:

> He established many deer preserves
> and he set up many laws concerning them,
> such that whoever killed a hart or a hind
> should be blinded.
> He forbade (hunting of) harts
> and also of boars.
> He loved the wild deer
> And he also decreed that the hares
> should be allowed to run free.
> His great men complained of it,
> and his poor men lamented it;
> but he was so severe
> that he ignored all their needs.

The Forest Laws were there to protect all aspects of the Forest, both the vert (French for green, meaning the plants and vegetation) and the venison (the game). So it was that you could commit an offence under either of these – trespass against the vert, or trespass against venison. However, the term 'protect' here is used in somewhat of a different sense than it is used today. Now, when we say protect, we are talking from a wildlife and environmental point of view, trying to keep the forest natural and pure, William though wanted it preserved for his hunt.

At one time it was believed that the Forest Laws actually dated back to King Canute. However, the document that suggests he created the laws was found to be a fake, and the first genuine record of Forest Law occurs in the Assize of Woodstock, 1184 – but these were clearly just a restatement and not an enactment of them.

Trespass against the vert consisted of many small, punishable offences. For example it was an offence to cut any timber, at all, except with the supervision of a forester, an agent of the Crown. But there were two more serious types of trespass: 'purpresture', the enclosure of land or the erection of buildings and 'assarting', the clearing of land. These laws applied to all lands within the Forest, even those not owned by the Crown.

Trespassing against the venison resulted in severe penalties, as the above poem suggests, though reports on punishments differ somewhat. Some suggest hands being chopped off or even being blinded just for shooting and missing (guaranteeing you would never shoot at another animal). Killing one of the King's deer was met with blinding or even death. Losing one's hands or one's vision was a high price to pay, especially as this was in a time when bringing home the bacon literally meant putting food on the table, so the loss of your hands or your sight would totally remove your ability to gain any kind of income.

The protection of the game did not just extend to the commoners not killing the deer; other restrictions were also imposed upon them. It was not even legal to possess bows and arrows lest they be used against the deer, and any dogs had to be kept lamed so they would not chase the deer. Hunting, of any kind, was also outlawed at night, to ensure the deer had peace and safety.

The enforcing of the law was undertaken by two main groups – the verderers, who were specific to the Forest, and from 1238 the Justice in Eyre who were, for matters of the Forest and the Forest alone, the highest court in the land. The latter group would travel between all of the Royal Forests, dispensing judgement where the verderers were unable to do so and passing sentence. This is where they got their name from, Eyre from the old French *errer* for 'journey'. The last known instance of the court being held in the New Forest was in the years 1669 to 1670, but even before this the laws had been much relaxed.

The verderers (again coming from the French *vert* for green) date back to medieval times, with early evidence showing that they were elected by the county but had the backing of the Crown. They would deal with the day-to-day affairs and minor offences usually by the application of fines, they did not have sentencing powers themselves so anything more serious would be referred upwards. The Charter of the Forest, in 1217, was an important document that went a long way to fixing the damage that had been done by the enactment of such harsh penalties and laws following on from the creation of the Forest. The laws that had made previous monarchs so unpopular were relaxed; offences were no longer punishable by mutilation or death, some recent additions to the Forest (afforested land) were returned, and a little more freedom was granted to private land. Anyone who was previously exiled was also allowed to return home. On top of this, rights of common (see below) were protected and enshrined in law. However, these changes did not go far enough to fix all the problems and some would not be resolved for hundreds of years.

Originally the verderers would sit on two different courts. The first, the Court of Attachment, dealt with any attachments made by officials of the Forest as well as assigning rights and swearing in Forest officials. As previously mentioned though, they could only deal with minor incidences with a maximum fine of 4*d* being imposed. The second court was the Court of Swanimote, which dealt with the pannage of pigs and the application of fence month and winter heying (where the Right of Pasture was removed – see below).

In the case of a deer being killed, an investigation would be undertaken, known as an inquisition; it was a thorough and serious affair. The arrow would be given to the verderers as evidence while the accused would be held in jail until the Court of Eyre could be convened. The body of the deer would be given to a spittal house (a house for the sick) or to the poor while the head of the deer went to the nearest town's freemen (those who were not tied to land under serfdom – a type of slavery). But it was not just killing a deer that was an offence; even after the reforms anyone who attempted to kill a deer would be punished as if they had taken its life. There were four different ways in which someone could be caught for illegally killing or trying to kill a deer:

Dog draw – having already wounded the deer, they are following it with a dog to try and capture it.
Stable stand – ready to shoot the deer, or hounds ready to be released at the deer.
Back bare – the deer is dead and being carried away.
Bloody hand – found in suspicious circumstances with blood on their person; literally caught red-handed.

Asserts and purpresture, trespasses against the vert, were investigated by regarders, who would visit the Forest every three years. Any trespasses found would be reported to the verderers. The regarders, the forerunners to foresters, were also the ones who would 'law the dogs'; this was the laming of the dog, often by removing three toes from the forefeet, to stop them from chasing deer. However, a quick bribe would often be enough to ensure your dog was left alone. There are though tales of regarders blowing their horns as they went through towns, causing any concealed dogs to bark. This mutilation was only applied to any dog of sufficient size to harm the deer – it is said that the Stirrup of Rufus would be used to see if the dog was large enough; if they could pass through it they would be left be. The Stirrup of Rufus actually dates from Tudor times and still resides in the Verderers Hall.

The New Forest verderers still exist today, though, of course, their role has changed greatly over the last 900 years. Their powers increased during the seventeenth and eighteenth centuries in relation to the navy's need for timber – this mainly meant the creation of powers for the planting and preservation of oaks. New offences were introduced, including such things as breaking inclosure fences – it was important to keep animals away from land in which there were newly growing trees, while stronger powers to deal with trespassers were also introduced to the same affect.

But it was in 1877 that the Court of the Verderers was properly modernised, with the passing of the New Forest Act of Parliament, also known as the Commoner's Charter. The oath of allegiance to the Crown was abolished, even though the Official Verderer was still appointed by the monarch. Then five additional ones would be chosen by commoners and Parliamentary voters within the parishes of the New Forest.

Further reforms were made in the New Forest Act of 1949, adding an additional four appointed verderers. Their powers were increased to include the creation and amendment of bylaws, many of which are in force today, to help the coexistence of the Forest, the inhabitants and the thousands upon thousands of people who visit the Forest each year.

Today there are ten verderers, five of whom are elected by those whose names appear on the Forest's own electoral register – to be on this list an inhabitant of the Forest must occupy at least one acre of land with common rights attached (see p. 38 for a list of common rights). To be elected as a verderer the candidate must occupy at least an acre with the right of pasture. Elections take place every three years, alternating between two and three being voted in, meaning that verderers serve on the court for six years in total. The post, an integral part of the Forest, is entirely voluntary.

The Chairman of the Court, the Official Verderer, is still appointed by the Crown whilst the remaining four are appointed by DEFRA (Department for the Environment, Food and Rural Affairs), the Forestry Commission, The National Park Authority and the Countryside Agency.

They are in charge of overseeing commoning and the court meets in open session the third Wednesday of every month followed by private committee – though today the two courts from medieval times exist as one, with any distinctions between them having long been lost. Any decision that will affect the Forest must be passed by them before it goes forward. Anyone can address the court verbally so long as it is accompanied in writing as well; this is known as a presentment. The Head Agister (see below) takes on the role of Crier of the Court, announcing on its commencement from the ancient oak dock, 'Oyez, Oyez, All manners of persons who have any presentment to make or matter or thing to do at this Court of Verderers; let them come forward and they shall be heard. God save the Queen.' The word 'presentment' dates back to the original role of the verderers when offences would be presented to them on which they had to pass judgement.

One thing which has remained constant, at least for a fair while, is the location where the court is held. The Verderers Hall, built around the Royal Manor of Lyndhurst in 1388, now known as Queen's House, has been the court's venue for hundreds of years.

Agisters are another important group of people in the Forest, a role that has also existed since medieval times, when they were also known as marksmen – it referred specifically to the management of pasturage in the Royal Forests. Part of their role was to collect fees from 'strangers' (people who wanted to graze their animals but had no right to do so). Their name comes from the word 'agist', which means to take livestock to graze for payment. Today five are appointed and employed by the verderers to look after commoners' stock and follow other instructions issued by the court. Each one will have their own area of the forest to look after, where they supervise all of the commonable animals. They must be highly skilled in animal welfare and riding, not to mention being in possession of an intimate knowledge of the Forest and where any of the commoners' stock are likely to be. Sadly one of their most frequent tasks is dealing with animals that have been involved in collisions with cars. Due to the suffering that these animals will undoubtedly be enduring it is often necessary to put the animals down – each agister is issued with a humane killer and is authorised to put the animals down if it is deemed the right thing to do to spare their suffering. Usually agisters are commoners who have spent most of their life working in the forest as it is a demanding job that requires years of skills. They work full time and are on call twenty-four hours a day – unlike the verderers it is a paid position.

Every summer they collect the marking fee, the payment a commoner must make in exchange for them turning their stock out into the Forest – this largely goes to pay their wages. On top of this they are to report on any violations of bylaws. Their most spectacular duty occurs once every year when they conduct the Pony Drifts, a round up of all the New Forest ponies (see the section below on New Forest ponies for more information on this).

Commoners

Commoners have been part of the New Forest since its creation in 1079 and they have played a vital role in its evolution. When you see ponies, donkeys or cattle in the National Park you are seeing commoners' stock and the art of commoning in action – it is them and their animals that have helped to shape the Forest into what it is today.

Commoners are those people who live in the Forest who have certain rights over the Forest attached to their land or properties – that is to say they must own or rent land that has common rights. Often this will remain within families as land is passed on from parents to children, with commoning often being a family tradition – but as society moves forward fewer and fewer people are taking up the rights attached to their land. Nowadays there is little, if any, money to be made from it so more and more are drawn to different careers.

In 1909 the New Forest Commoners Defence Association (CDA) was formed to deal with the conflict that was arising between the increasing urban population around the forest and the commoners and their animals. They have been involved in many activities over the last century; in the 1920s they paid for the installation of telephones in the homes of agisters so that they could be informed of animal injuries, particularly road related, more quickly. They have taken part in many campaigns (such as 40mph speed limits on minor roads) and it was they who developed the reflective collars that are now given out by verderers for free to help make animals more visible. In 2007 they started to address the dwindling number of young people who are taking on the ancient art of communing.

As the result of consultation following a review, a Young Commoners group was established, with three main aims: raising the profile of young commoners, increasing their participation both in commoning and decision making in the Forest, gaining back-up grazing to support their commoning activity and education. A Colts Council has also been established which is made up of a group of under sixteens involved in commoning, it will support them with training and knowledge as well as social activities.

There are six types of right:

The Right of Common Pasture – This is probably the most important right both for the commoners and the Forest. It allows commoners to turn out their ponies, cattle, donkeys and mules onto the common grazing land. Commoners wanting to take up this right must register with the Verderers' Clerk, who will confirm their right exists and allocate a brand to them. When the fee (the marking fee) is paid they are free to turn out their stock.

It is most likely that this right arose as a form of compensation when the Forest was created. So as to not interfere with the Hunt fences were not allowed, nor was the cultivation of any new land, making things hard for locals trying to survive off the land. Hence the Right of Pasture was created, though originally it was not an all-year affair, with certain parts of the year being restricted. The first was known as Fence Month and was between 20 June and 20 July when does would normally give birth to their fawns. The second was during winter and was called heying (or winter heying) when the right could be withdrawn if food was scare. This was so that the deer would have enough to eat and their population would not decline – again in an effort to retain the Forest as a hunting reserve.

The Right of Common of Mast – This is where pigs may be turned out during pannage season. This occurs during the autumn and lasts for a minimum of sixty days. A privileged sow (one that is pregnant) can, upon application, be allowed to graze outside this time although they must return at night. It is an important and essential right for the Forest as the pigs can digest acorns to no ill effect, whereas large quantities can be harmful to other animals – resulting in the death of both ponies and cattle. Until the New Forest Act of 1964 the season was fixed from 25 September to 22 November, but if the acorns fell late pigs started invading local gardens so the dates were made flexible, decided by the verderers.

The Right of Common of Sheep – This is the right to turn out sheep, though this is an unusual right that is rarely exercised.

The Rights of Common of Marl – Marl is the right to dig a special type of clay that is good for agricultural land. This can be taken from twenty-three different pits throughout the forest, but is currently not taken advantage of as modern agricultural methods have made it unnecessary.

The Right of Common Turbary – This is the right to cut turf for burning within their homes – for every one cut two adjacent ones have to be left, to stop stripping of any one area. Just like the right of Marl this is not currently exercised.

The Right of Common of Fuelwood – Formerly called the Right of Estovers it is the right to fuel wood, which today means that the Forestry Commission must give them a specified number of cords of wood (a stack of wood 8ft long, 4ft high and 4ft deep). There are only around 100 houses with this right. Any wood allocated must be burnt within the home.

There are around 800 houses and smallholdings to which common rights are attached, though about only half of the owners exercise these rights in the New Forest. All rights are recorded in the New Forest Atlas which anyone can look through or request a search of. This was compiled after the 1964 New Forest Act. Even though these rights have been around long before even William the Conqueror any that were unclaimed by 1964 have been lost.

New Forest stock

Each year the number of stock in the New Forest varies. In 2008, however, there were 4,485 ponies, 2,566 cattle, 127 donkeys, 439 pigs and a mere 62 sheep owned by around 500 commoners.

New Forest Ponies – You can never guarantee seeing anything in the New Forest, or at least anything that moves, but you would have to be incredibly unlucky not to see one of the 4,500 New Forest ponies that are dotted around the forest, whether you are on open heath, woodland or in town you can see them over almost the entire ground that the New Forest covers. You will notice a few things about them straight away. There are a lot of them; some appear to be wild whilst some wear reflective collars. More often than not

One of the ubiquitous New Forest ponies.

they will be eating or just ambling along, often totally oblivious to any disruption they my be causing to traffic – the more cynical amongst you might even think they enjoy walking in the middle of the road; they certainly do not take much notice of any cars. They are generally docile though they are semi-wild and should not be touched or fed by the public. Feeding them encourages them to approach car parks and roads where they will be at further risk of road traffic accidents.

Ponies in the New Forest come in a variety of different shapes, sizes and colours – but a New Forest pony is a particular breed; it is one of the mountain and moorland breeds of ponies that are native to the British Isles.

Are they wild? The short answer is no, they are owned by commoners, though many of them live wild in the Forest and rarely leave it – they will graze on the Forest lawns in the summer and on the heath in the winter. So whilst they are not technically wild they do lead an almost wild life. People often think that the ones with reflective collars are less wild, but they are put on simply as a measure to protect the animals that graze in areas of unenclosed land adjacent to unfenced roads as they are the ones most at risk of being hit by vehicles. This is also why all minor roads in the New

Forest have a speed limit of 40mph, and it is also why it is important for you to stick to them. Sadly a lot of animals are killed by traffic each year.

Usually the ponies will stick within a half-mile radius, though not necessarily anywhere near the commoner that owns them. The ponies are between 120 and 148cm in height and are usually bay, chestnut or grey, however they can be any colours except piebald (black and white patches), skewbald (white and non-black colour patches) and cremello (pale creamish skin and blue eyes).

Ponies have been around in Britain since time immemorial, but over the course of history they have been bred away from their ancestral archetype. The first reference to the New Forest pony as a separate breed was in 1016, but the first stud book was not until 1910 some 900 years later, and in between these two dates, and right up until 1930, the species has undergone some large changes. Some of these were through the deliberate introduction of other types of pony in attempts at improvement, whilst some would have undoubtedly been from the natural comings and goings of people and their ponies within the forest.

The first known instance of such improvement was by King Henry III (1207-1272), who introduced Welsh ponies into the Forest. Henry VIII (1491-1547), in a slightly crueller streak, ordered all of the small ponies killed off, in a move that he hoped would lead to a larger, stronger pony. The next recorded instance of improving the breed was in 1756 when a famous thoroughbred stallion called Masque was released, and then between 1852 to 1860 Queen Victoria lent one of her Arab stallions, named Zorah, into the Forest.

In 1891 the Association for the Improvement of the New Forest pony was founded and in 1893 Lord Arthur Cecil started importing specimens from Dartmoor, Exmoor, the Fells, the Highlands and Wales. The year 1906 saw the formation of the Burley and District New Forest Pony and Cattle Breeding Society, which took on the role of improving the breed – it was they who started the stud book in 1910. Twenty years later it was decided that no more outside blood would be introduced and the breed would be kept pure. In 1960 the New Forest Pony Breeding and Cattle Breeding Society was formed which keeps its own stud book.

Most of the ponies in the forest are mares, although there are few geldings (male but castrated), which means that breeding is highly controlled. Today, to try and keep the stock pure, only stallions that have been passed by the verderers are allowed into the Forest.

New Forest ponies are well known for their friendliness, strength and quickness to learn. Their smaller stature makes them ideal for children to ride, whereas a large adult might have trouble. They are such a popular breed that New Forest Pony Societies exists in most Northern European countries as well as in Australia and America.

Even though New Forest ponies are virtually feral, they are still owned by commoners and as such they require looking after as well as accounting for. To this end, each year the Pony Drifts occur. This is a huge undertaking where all of the New Forest ponies are rounded up and checked. People both on horseback and on foot gather up all of the ponies in autumn, between the start of August and the start of November, into groups ranging from 30 to 200 ponies. In all, around 200 of these drifts are held, with agisters and commoners alike helping in the process. The police will also give a hand, dealing mostly with traffic, whilst the Forestry Commission help out with other members of the public, making sure that there are as few problems as possible. The drifts usually start at either eight or ten in the morning, and the ponies are rounded up into large pens. From there four or five are taken into a smaller pen, called a pound where it is far easier to deal with them. Agisters will then check their welfare, giving worming treatment if necessary after which the Agisters will put a small cut into their tail hair to show that they have been seen to – this is also to check that the marking fee for each animal has been paid. The pattern that is cut into each animal is unique to the agister, that way it is known who dealt with each one. In the event that the pony is not deemed healthy enough to be let go, the agister will see to it that it is kept until it has returned to full health. The commoners also can choose to keep some animals at home for the winter, usually the foals – these animals are also hot branded to show who they are owned by.

Each commoner has their own brand, usually based on their initials, each of which can be seen on a barn door which was created in 1988 to commemorate the opening of the New Forest Museum in Lyndhurst by HRH the Duke of Edinburgh.

It is also at this time that the reflective collars are fitted, around 800 to 1,000 are fitted each year, and they are generously paid for by the verderers. Some ponies are also kept back to sell. Members of the public are not allowed to take part in the drifts, and are discouraged from attempting to view the proceedings as the ponies are semi-wild and certainly can move at pace when being herded – this can make it dangerous for those who are not used to the drift and do not know how to deal with ponies. On top of this

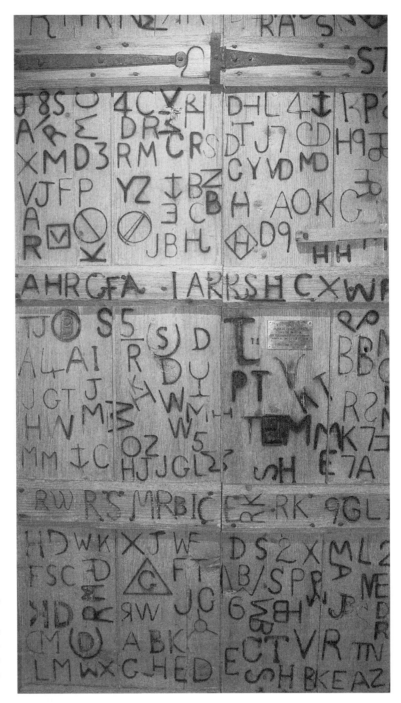

This door can be seen in the New Forest Museum, each of the markings on it are the brandings used by the commoners to mark their stock.

The site of the pony sales at Beaulieu Road Yard.

sometimes a lot of effort can be wasted as the ponies can be spooked and will not remain under the control of the people herding them, negating hours of work rounding them up. Spectators became such a problem that in 2007 that the verderers stopped publishing the locations and times for the drifts, intended for those involved in the proceedings, on their website. They also, in the same year, made a request to the general public – unless you are directly involved, please stay away!

At several other times throughout the year, there are pony sales that are held at the Beaulieu Road Yard, opposite Beaulieu Road station, where they are often bought as riding ponies for their versatility.

After the drift all the ponies are released and most of them will then remain wild for the next twelve months. Some, however, will have a little more contact.

Once a year a race is held, usually on Boxing Day. The night before the race the commoners taking part will be given the start and finishing points – there is no set route, meaning that a good knowledge of the Forest is essential. More often than not different people will take different routes through the forest in an attempt to be the first one to cross the finishing line.

The other breed of pony that you are likely to encounter on your travels is the well known Shetland pony, which are much smaller than their New Forest relatives and are at most 107cm tall. They are also easily spotted by their short legs and heavy coats.

New Forest ponies have played an important roll in shaping the New Forest, and are of particular importance to heather and heathland, where they stop the grass from overgrowing and swamping it – it is for this reason that they are often referred to as the architects of the forest. In fact, they are so successful at doing this that in 2009 a herd of New Forest ponies was sent to Sherwood Forest to help protect the heathland there.

But of course the New Forest pony is not the only animal in the forest, and the commoners own several other creatures as well.

Pigs – Whilst pigs are not generally seen roaming around the New Forest there are still a large number of them and they play an important role. During autumn they are released to graze in the Forest, where they eat thousands of acorns that are potentially harmful to the ponies. In the nineteenth century up to 6,000 pigs were turned out, but in recent times it has been between 200 and 600. Traditionally it was an opportunity for commoners to fatten up their pigs for slaughter.

Unlike ponies they are not branded, instead an identity tag is placed in its ear and a ring is put through its nose to reduced the damage they do by rooting.

Whilst pigs are generally quite docile and used to people, they can occasionally be aggressive, and have even known to do rather odd things as shown by the news extract below. But it is just another reminder that you are best off leaving animals in peace and letting them get on with their business!

The adorable-looking Shetland pony.

A rogue pig charged at a woman rider in the New Forest causing her horse to spook and buck her off. The pig then pushed the woman into a thorny hedge and tried to bite her legs. She was saved by a dog walker who not only chased off the pig but caught her frightened horse. The woman was taken to hospital but later released with broken ribs.

The pigs found here are of various breeds but the original New Forest breed, the Wessex Saddleback, is now extinct in the UK.

Cattle – There are also several species of cattle that can be found wandering around the Forest. The most common are Galloway – named after the Galloway region of Scotland – but by far the most distinctive cattle you will see are of the Highland variety, with their long curved horns. You can also see Hereford, Dexter (the smallest European breed of cattle – half the size of the Hereford), Kerry and the British White.

The number of cattle in the Forest in the summer is much larger (around 2,500) than in the winter; during the colder months there is less in the way of grazing and many of the cattle have to return to their owners' holdings. Generally they are bred for their meat. Usually calving takes place at the commoner's holdings in case there is a problem, as being on hand can alleviate many of the complications that can arise. They will often also be removed

One of the many highland cattle that can be seen roaming the Forest.

Donkeys are often spotted nearer to towns than ponies are.

in autumn to prevent them from eating acorns, which are highly poisonous to them. Another malady that cattle can suffer from is Red Water Disease, caused by the ticks carried by deer; it is fatal if left untreated. New Forest bred cattle acquire a natural immunity, but cattle brought in from the outside are most at risk.

Cows are very docile, but as with all animals care should be taken, especially if there are calves around as a mother can often be very protective.

Donkeys – Only around 100 donkeys are turned out into the Forest, but they are often seen around the villages. They are hardier than the ponies, rarely needing to return to the commoner's holdings for the winter. Their hooves, however, need regular trimming lest they become lame. Another difference compared with the ponies is that jacks (male donkeys) are allowed to roam the forest all year round. A donkey foal is worth around £500, twice as much as a pony's.

Sheep – As previously mentioned, commoners' sheep are particularly rare in the New Forest, and at the time of writing, there is only one commoner who exercises the right to turn sheep out – you can find them on the National Trust owned commons around Bramshaw.

❧ DEATH IN THE FOREST ❧

It was beautiful, a full twelve tines on its antlers. A kill that any huntsmen would be proud of. The stag hadn't noticed him there. Quietly but quickly he drew an arrow, he got an almost imperceptible nod from William, the King was saying take the shot. He nocked the bow, and pulled the string back hard, until it was past his nose. The target was in sight, one good shot would be all it needed – wounding the deer would simply be cruel, one shot was all it needed. One shot is all he would take.

He loosed the arrow but disaster struck, his horse had moved. It had only been a fraction but enough to alert the deer and throw his shot. It ricocheted off a giant oak just to the deer's left.

Never mind, there were more deer in the forest and plenty more sport for today. He turned to face William, but he was not on his horse. Quickly dismounting he approached the body on the ground. The arrow had pierced his heart. The King was already dead.

Panic filled his heart, he couldn't stay here, they would surely accuse him of murder. He would be tortured and killed – treason was not taken lightly. He certainly couldn't stay in the country, he would have to go. Leaving the King's body where it had fallen he mounted his steed with Normandy, and the safety of foreign shores, in his mind.

Hunting, as is to be expected, was a dangerous activity, and not just for the animals being chased. Stags could charge with their sharp antlers, boars, when cornered, could be aggressive and vicious – no animal will willingly lay down its life to die, and after the chase of the hunt they knew exactly what was coming. But it was not just the animals that made hunting in the New Forest such a dangerous place, not when there were bows being drawn and arrows being fired – many a hunting accident would occur over the Forest's long history. Moreover the New Forest was a particularly unlucky place for William the Conqueror's descendants with two of his children, and one illegitimate grandson, meeting an unwholesome end amongst the trees.

The first to die was Richard, the second son of William the Conqueror. He was often incorrectly referred to as the Duke of Bernay, due to a misinterpretation of his tombstone. After numerous troubles between William and his eldest son Robert, Richard was first in line for the throne. Yet on a trip to visit England in 1081 his hopes of ever taking the throne were brought to an abrupt end when he was killed in a hunting accident. Richard's mauling, supposedly by a stag, left William Rufus as the emergent heir. Richard was later buried at Winchester Cathedral. The finger of suspicion has been pointed at Henry. He was Richard's younger brother and therefore in direct line for the throne – but he was merely twelve or thirteen at the time. Some say at such a young age this sort of treachery and plotting is unlikely, yet after another so called hunting accident almost twenty years later Henry would become King.

The second to go was William the Conqueror's grandson. During the period of his life as a travelling knight Robert, William's eldest son, had two illegitimate children. One of them was named Richard and he spent much time in the court of William Rufus, who had taken the throne in 1087. Just like his uncle of the same name he was killed, in 1099, in hunting accident in the New Forest.

But it did not stop there. In 1100 a further accident occurred. William II, King of the English, better known as William Rufus (probably for his reddish complexion and hair) had been on the thrown for a mere thirteen years when he was killed, almost instantly, by an arrow through the heart, or possibly the lung (again, sources differ as to how he was killed, though generally they agree that it was quick and that it was by an arrow). In one version of events William was with Sir Walter Tyrrell in the New Forest when the two of them were separated from the rest of the hunters. Then, having sighted the deer, William took the first shot and missed, Tyrrell took the second, missing the stag but killing the King. Seeing William dead and fearing the blame that would undoubtedly fall on his shoulders, he fled to Normandy, beyond the reach of the English nobles. There is some doubt over whether Tyrrell would have missed a shot so badly, he was considered the best shot in the court, and another contemporary source, Orderic Vitalis, claims that William gave the two sharpest arrows to Tyrrell, a fitting bequest for the man who was the deadliest shot. One tale even tells of how Tyrrell, upon fleeing, stopped to have his horse re-shod, with the horseshoes being put on backwards in order to confuse anyone who gave chase. A chase that never happened.

William was not a much-loved King, with the contemporary Anglo-Saxon Chronicles going as far to say, 'Hated by almost all his people.' He was considered a ruthless ruler, he had issues with the Church and he seemed to scorn England and its culture at every opportunity. On top of this he had continued and, in many ways worsened, the harsh Forest Laws that his father had set up.

With no wife or children, legitimate or otherwise, that left his brothers – Henry and the currently crusading Robert – as contenders for the kingdom.

In the ensuing chaos the nobles rushed back to their own lands; with no King there was no law, it was each to their own. They had to look after their lands and their property, lest they lose out themselves. Henry rushed to Winchester, the location of the Royal Treasury – essential if he was going to secure the throne – and within days he was in London to be crowned, even though it was his absent brother, Robert, who was the rightful heir. Despite vigorous protests from William de Breteuille, who had ridden to Winchester to claim the throne for Robert, it was on 5 August, just three days later, that Henry became Henry I, the new King of England.

What seems to have been overlooked in the turmoil was the body being attended to. As legend has it the body was found the next day by a group of peasants and that a charcoal burner by the name of Purkis took the King's body on his cart to Winchester Cathedral, the final resting place of the red-faced King.

It may well have been an accident. There was never any attempt to bring Walter Tyrrell to justice, suggesting that the act may have simply been a hunting trip gone wrong – why punish someone who was innocent? He certainly, years later, denied ever being with the King when he died – but then of course denial is not necessarily a sign of innocence. He did not even lose his lands in England and his brothers-in-law prospered under the new King, even though they too were in the hunting party. But perhaps this lack of reprisal against him signified something more sinister. Perhaps he was a scapegoat, or maybe a willing participant in a plot to remove William and supplant Henry on the throne – it does seem unlikely that Henry, who was part of the hunting party, managed to organise a coronation in a just a few days, something that would be hard to accomplish if planned well in advance let alone at such short notice. And the timing of his other brother being on a crusade was more than just a little fortuitous for him.

Other, less mainstream theories have even suggested that William Rufus went voluntarily to his death to atone for the sins of his people as a sacrificial victim, though there is no evidence to support this idea. Some historians even put a romantic twist on the whole affair, with William Rufus being killed for the love of a lady. The lady in question was Eadgyth, daughter of the King of Scotland and great-great-granddaughter or Edmund Ironside, an early English King. Rufus had made advances on her, making his intentions clear to all. To protect her from this, her aunt the Abbess Christina, whose care she was under, dressed her as nun in Romsey Abbey, where they were staying. This deception helped to keep her safely out of reach of Rufus, whose reputation was not an endearing one. Not only did this keep her safe from Rufus, but also out of reach of Henry. Yet when Henry did come to the throne after Rufus' untimely death, he did indeed marry her, with her becoming Queen Matilda. Not only did he have a quick marriage but when he had approached the Archbishop about them being wed he talked of his long-standing love for her – meaning his love must have pre-dated his crowning as they only married on the 11 November, just a few months after the incident in the New Forest. If this had been the case, then with Rufus on the throne any romantic involvement, let alone marriage, would have been impossible, for the law at the time started and stopped with the King. So maybe, just maybe, Rufus died for love.

Whether the death was an accident or something more sinister may never be known, but it was the third hunting-related death in the family.

On one of the walks in the forest you can get a little bit closer to these events and visit the Rufus Stone – the most recent of which was erected in 1841 – a cast-iron 'stone' that marks the supposed spot where he fell. The stone is located near to the Sir Walter Tyrrell pub near the town of Brook. The exact location of his death, just as the circumstances surrounding it, are unclear, with recent evidence suggesting he may have fallen somewhere nearer Beaulieu.

The inscriptions themselves tell a story of one version of events:

Here stood the oak tree on which an arrow shot by Sir Walter Tyrrell at a stag, glanced and struck King William the Second, surnamed Rufus, on the breast, of which he instantly died, on the second day of August, anno 1100.

King William the Second, surnamed Rufus being slain, as before related, was laid in a cart, belonging to one Purkis, and drawn from hence, to Winchester, and buried in the Cathedral Church of that city.

That the spot where an event so memorable might not hereafter be forgotten, the enclosed stone was set up by John Lord Delaware who had seen the tree growing in this place. This stone having been much mutilated, and the inscriptions on each of its three sides defaced. This more durable memorial with the original inscriptions was erected in the year 1841, by WM Sturges Bourne, Warden.

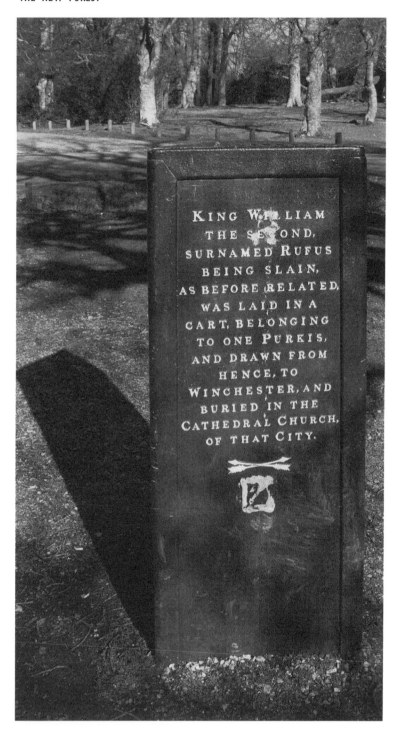

KING WILLIAM
THE SECOND,
SURNAMED RUFUS
BEING SLAIN,
AS BEFORE RELATED,
WAS LAID IN A
CART, BELONGING
TO ONE PURKIS,
AND DRAWN FROM
HENCE, TO
WINCHESTER, AND
BURIED IN THE
CATHEDRAL CHURCH,
OF THAT CITY.

The Rufus Stone, marking the spot where it is believed that William Rufus fell.

Not just royalty

Of course, it was not just royalty that died in the forest, and deaths did not just occur during those first formative years. If you are willing to take the time you can spot a few names you may know amongst the gravestones of the New Forest, and a few names that, while they may not be familiar, are of significance.

Alice Hargreaves – Born Alice Liddell she is generally considered to be the inspiration for *Alice's Adventures in Wonderland* by Lewis Carroll. Lewis Carroll was the pen name of Charles Lutwidge Dodgson, who met the Liddell family in 1855. He would take Alice and two of her sisters on boating trips and picnics around Oxford, where they all lived. During these trips he would tell them stories and he would take numerous photos of them, getting them to dress up in different costumes. To what degree the book is based on her is, just like their real-life relationship, open to much debate, but the books are dedicated to her and they are set on her birthday, the 4 May and her half birthday 4 November. There are other things dotted around the book, such as an acrostic poem which spells out her full name. She spent the end of her life in and around Lyndhurst, with her body being buried at the Church of St Michael and All Angels, Lyndhurst.

Sir Arthur Conan Doyle – Best known for the creation of Sherlock Holmes, he was a writer and a doctor. His works, however, go far beyond that of detective stories including works of science fiction, historical novels, plays, poetry and non-fiction. He was also deeply interested in spiritualism and the supernatural, perhaps even drawn in part to the New Forest by the tales of witchcraft whispered amongst the trees. He died on 7 July 1930 of a heart attack at the age of seventy-one. He was buried next to his second wife in the churchyard at Minstead. The epitaph reads:

STEEL TRUE
BLADE STRAIGHT
ARTHUR CONAN DOYLE
KNIGHT
PATRIOT, PHYSICIAN & MAN OF LETTERS

Augustus John – Born on 4 January 1878 in Wales, he was an important painter in the post-impressionistic movement. In the 1920s he was Britain's leading portrait painter, having done paintings of important figures such as Thomas Hardy, W.B. Yeats,

George Bernard Shaw and Dylan Thomas. He spent the later part of his life in Fordinbridge, where he worked until his death in 1961.

William Gipling – Picturesque may well be a word that you would use about the New Forest, but it was a term that was first defined by Gilpin in 1768 is his *Essays on Prints* – he talked about 'that kind of beauty which is agreeable in picture'. Unlike his brother, though, he was not a professional painter, instead taking up a career in the church and then as a headmaster. In later life, starting in 1777, he became vicar of Boldre in the New Forest, where, it its churchyard you can see his grave. He died in 1804 at the age of eighty.

🌺 THE FOREST AT WAR 🌺

The news had come back. It seemed that fate had struck and it hadn't struck on their side. The news had been disastrous, the German army had outmanoeuvred them, the entire British Expeditionary Force was cut off from the main French force; they were trapped, flanked on either side by the Germans. Over 100,000 men, not to mention all of the French soldiers too, were facing certain defeat which meant capture or death. But they weren't dead yet. And the Brits had a plan.

He looked out over Calshot Spit and at his plane, they had practised for this, if his sea plane couldn't evacuate a few soldiers then what was the point, what was any of this good for? This wasn't just going to be the miracle of the small ships, not if he had anything to do with it – it was going to be the miracle of his sea plane too.

He set off, leaving the New Forest behind him – the flight over was nerve-racking, they had been told what to expect but nothing can prepare you for real combat, for real war, no matter what anyone says or does it's not the same.

The Belgian coast came into view, and a couple of minutes after that the port of Dunkirk was clear, at least what was left of it. He flew in low, the RAF high above fending off the Luftwaffe as much as they could – they set down on the sea, mercifully calm for them today. Soldiers scrambled into the plane, some of them had been waiting in the water for hours, unsure if they would be getting their turn, if they would get their evacuation. With as many people as he'd dare carry he set off back to England, to safety. But he knew as soon as he was back he would just turn around again, while there were British troops left, his plane would stay in the air.

During England's history she has often been at war, but not since 1066 has she been conquered. With the First World War in 1914 and sadly then again in 1939 for the Second World War it was all hands on deck, with everyone and every part of the country doing their bit for the war effort, for King and country. But the New Forest's relationship with war began a long time before the assassination of an archduke or Germany's invasion of Poland.

On some levels the New Forest has always been involved in war, its very purpose was for hunting game. The Normans unashamedly admitted that one of the aims of hunting was to hone one's skills for war (*see* 'The Hunt'). But the Forest was a lot more than a mere game reserve. Even as early as 1379 records show that its wood was being used for fortifications in various places, including Southampton, Portsmouth and the Isle of Wight.

In 1611 the Royal Navy requested 1,800 oaks for ship building and soon this arrangement became more regular when from about 1670 a small amount of timber was taken each year, around 300 oaks and 100 beech – though records are sketchy on how much was felled as much of the timber was stolen by the carpenters working on the ships. Three hundred acres were also planted at this time, and there was some conflict between the need for wood and the preservation of the area for hunting.

With an increasing number of ships being built more wood was needed, and this meant that the navy needed to know how many trees there were available. To this end a survey was conducted by the navy in 1707 which showed that there were 12,476 trees suitable for ship building within the Forest. In a previous, non-military survey of 1608 there had been 123,927 trees which were shown as suitable. Their ships required mature oaks in their construction and with much more wood being used for charcoal in the iron industry, as well as for day-to-day construction, the navy was rightly worried about its supplies.

Towards the end of the seventeenth century much oak was wasted – it was oak above all else that was considered best for shipbuilding – John Evelyn, a contemporary expert on trees wrote what was considered the first published text on forestry, the *Sylva, or A Discourse on Forest-Trees and the Propagation of Timber in His Majesty's Dominions*. It was published in 1662 by the Royal Society and had this to say about English Oak:

> It is then for the esteem which these wise and glorious people had
> of this tree above all others, that I will first begin with the oak; and

> indeed it carries it from all other timber whatsoever, for building of
> ships in general, and in particular being tough, bending well, strong
> and not too heavy, nor easily admitting water.

Oak takes around a hundred years to season, which is a considerable amount of time, so if there is a shortage there are no quick fixes – you either need to have a very large reserve of good, well-aged trees, or be able to predict your usage a hundred years in advance, something that is hardly possible. The Royal Navy made a significant error, deciding to use many unseasoned trees – not only did the constructed ships not last long but later down the line there were fewer mature oaks to be harvested, compounding the problem.

In an attempt to address this worrying shortage Parliament looked at the Royal Forests as an area to produce the much needed wood, and the 1698 New Forest Act put aside 2,000 acres to be planted immediately, with another 200 acres a year for the next twenty years. However, this was not put into action properly and over the next twenty years the supply remained low – in a fifty-year period only enough timber to meet four years of the navy's need was supplied.

Later surveys of 1764 and 1782 showed a steady improvement. However, the needs of the navy outstripped this until in 1808, when an extensive planting programme began, with 12,000 acres being planted over the next sixty years – but as oaks take so long to grow it was too late for the needs of the navy, which would soon dispense with wooden ships entirely.

Modern-day Beaulieu is better known for cars than it is for ships, yet it had been constructing vessels for defending our shores long before the invention of the car. Buckler's Hard is a small hamlet on the banks of the Beaulieu River, and it is now part of the 9,000 acre Beaulieu Estate. When it was originally built in the eighteenth century by the second duke of Montagu it was intended as a free port for trade with the West Indies. However, it was soon taken over to build ships for Admiral Nelson's fleet. Three of the ships constructed in the New Forest, the HMS *Euryalus* (376 guns), *Swiftsure* (74 guns) and *Agamemnon* (64 guns) fought in the Battle of Trafalgar in 1805. The latter of these needed over 2,000 mature oaks when it was constructed in 1781 and even this vast amount of wood still led to a ship that was considered small. The acquisition of timber accounted for about half the cost of a ship at the time, which during Napoleon's time was around £1,000 per gun – but often the repairs and upkeep over time could cause this to swell vastly, especially if lower quality, younger oak, was used. The timber was split into three types: mast and plank and compass (which was used for the curved hull and came from curved branches).

Even though Buckler's Hard built numerous ships (around fifty vessels between 1745 and 1818), the industry declined and eventually production stopped – but this would not be the last time that Buckler's Hard would play an important role during war time.

Visitor Information – There is a maritime museum at Buckler's Hard, see www.bucklershard.co.uk for details on opening times and admission prices.

In 1776, under King George III, a Royal Commission was set up to look at the state of the forests, in particular improving how much timber it could supply the navy, and up until 1862 a large amount of timber continued to be supplied from the New Forest. It was in then that ironclads started to be used, and with the peculiar exception of mine-sweeping ships in the Second World War (see below) it was the last time that the navy was in such need of New Forest timber.

Over the centuries so much wood was used, and the navy was so successful at defending our shores, that they are often referred to as 'the Wooden Walls of Old England', indeed their official quick march is 'Heart of Oak', and that heart was made of the New Forest.

The New Forest's geographical and strategic location on the South Coast led to the Forest having a significant role during the two world wars, the effect of which can still be seen. As the New Forest National Park Authority put it, during the wars, the New Forest was 'special for entirely different reasons'.

The First World War

A quick stroll around the Forest will belie the fact that this nature reserve was left untouched by the hardships of conflict. St Nicholas' Church, for example, has around 100 graves of some of the soldiers who died while receiving treatment from the wartime Brockenhurst Hospital – the vast majority (ninety-three) were from New Zealand. Many a large area and building were appropriated for the war effort; two hotels, the Forest Park Hotel and the Balmer Lawn Hotel were used as field hospitals (though the latter would get a much more prominent role during the Second World War). The Forest's close location to the south coast made it an ideal point for the receiving and setting off of troops.

In fact, it was the New Forest that was the staging point for troops destined for France, with much training occurring in the Forest. Just like the hunts of 800 years before, the Forest was used for honing military skill. Troops from all around the Empire and Commonwealth would gather in the New Forest, bringing numerous people from varying nationalities, an unusual sight for the New Forest – an article, printed in the *Times* on 28 October 1914, even remarks on the strange site of an area of the New Forest being covered with Indian troops, slightly older than their British counterparts, accompanied by mules.

The area around Bolton's Bench, near Lyndhurst, now considered a beauty spot, was used as a grenade training school. In an activity that would never be allowed in a National Park today, nor on any such endangered habitat, hundreds of soldiers were shown the art of tossing grenades – something that has definitely left its mark on the New Forest, even now, with areas of uneven ground still evident for someone with a keen eye. The area is named after the Duke of Bolton, who held the office of Master Keeper of Burley Baliwick during the eighteenth century.

Dogs have been considered man's best friends since time immemorial and during the First World War they took this to the extreme. On 9 December 1918 dogs of the war got a mention in the *Times* for the sterling work that they had been doing, also mentioned was the place where war dogs were trained: Lyndhurst.

The training and use of war dogs first started in early 1917 when the War Dog School of Instruction was founded, with Lieutenant Colonel Richardson at its head. He had spent most of his life training dogs for the military and the police, making him an ideal person to head up the school. The school was originally started in Shrewsbury but soon moved to Matley Wood, near Lyndhurst, where the woods, streams and open heath provided an ideal place for the dogs to be trained before they were sent off for war.

Gamekeepers, hunters and shepherds were recalled from the army to be instructed in the art of training the dogs, whilst the dogs themselves, at first, were taken from the Battersea, Birmingham and Liverpool Homes for Lost Dogs (thus saving many of them from being put down). In turn, the dogs saved the lives of many soldiers in the roles that they would undertake. One of the most important was that of messenger. These dogs were fit and agile, able to cover distances far quicker than a man could, with the added benefit of being much quieter and harder to spot – they could convey a message that would take a man an hour and a half in a mere twenty minutes –

a fact that without doubt saved numerous lives during the war. Other roles included sentry positions, where they were able to spot enemy units far sooner than a man could. Finally, they were also used as good old-fashioned guard dogs – not only were they well suited to this job but it allowed men to be freed up for other things. The dogs found most useful for this work were collies, Airedales and lurchers, with them all being well received by soldiers in the field.

As time went on, the school became highly successful with more dogs being needed. Although the police supplied stray dogs the eventual need led to an appeal to the public to donate their dogs – it was well met, with many a family pet doing its duty for King and country.

The trees were once more called upon to help the war effort with over 2,000 acres being felled – this went a large way to cover the fall of imports that occurred in the war (2.5 million tonnes of timber in 1918, as opposed to 6.5 million tons in 1916). The trees cut down were mostly broad-leaved deciduous, being replaced by fast growing conifers – something we would be grateful for during the next world war. Charcoal burning also made a return to the forest – the charcoal being used to make the absorbing material in gas masks.

The coast has always played an important role in Britain's defence, and the coastline of the New Forest is no different. Today you can go to Calshot and have a look at Calshot Castle, an artillery fortification constructed by Henry VIII to defend the coast, specifically the entrance to Southampton Water. It was constructed from stone taken from Beualieu Abbey and it was in use until 1956 – it is now an English Heritage site. Calshot Castle, along with Hurst Castle (another one of Henry VIII's so called Device Forts), formed part of the coastal defences that helped to keep Britain safe during both world wars.

In 1913, just before the outbreak of the war, Calshot Spit was taken over by the Royal Flying Corps, becoming Calshot Naval Air Station. Of the hangers built, the Sopworth Hangar, is the second oldest in Britain, whilst the largest, Sunderland Hangar (built in 1917), is still in use today as Calshot Activities Centre – here they have a climbing wall, dry-ski slope, a variety of water sports and even a velodrome. The air station was used for training, particularly focussing around the seaplane. Winston Churchill, then the First Lord of the Admiralty, was a great supporter and took his first trip on a seaplane there.

With the outbreak of war in 1914 and the changes that the Royal Navy made to the air branch, Calshot Naval Air Station became

Calshot Castle, defending the English coastline.

RNAS (Royal Navy Air Service) Calshot and the role of Calshot was extended to protecting shipping in the English Channel as well as taking part in coastal defence. On 1 April 1918 the Royal Air Force was formed and Calshot became the headquarters for Number 10 Group RAF. After the First World War it became home to the RAF School of Naval Co-operation and Aerial Navigation, being renamed RAF Base Calshot in 1922.

An airfield that had been created at East Boldre in 1910 was taken over by the War Department, with the training of pilots taking place from 1916.

The Coupe d'Aviation Maritime Jacques Schneider (or Schneider Trophy for short) was a race for seaplanes and was held eleven times between 1913 and 1931, with the final two races being held at Calshot and won by Britain – the advances made in plane design for these races proved invaluable and Calshot would once more play an important role in the Second World War.

The Second World War

Sadly the Forest did not have long to recover from the First World War before it was once again called upon to defend the nation, this time with a much greater effect on the landscape – much of which you can still see today.

The start of the war went badly for Europe; Germany's tactic of Blitzkrieg and the French faith in the impenetrability of the Ardennes allowed the Germans to outflank the Allies. The British Expeditionary Force was cut off from the main French force, and was surrounded with only one direction left to go, Dunkirk. It seemed like all was lost, Churchill described it as, 'a colossal military disaster,' and that, 'the whole root and core and the brain of the British army,' was about to be lost. All the Germans had to do was cut off the British retreat to Dunkirk, closing the port, and the entire force would have been lost. Yet Hitler did not take advantage of this, halting his troops for three days – long enough for Britain to plan an evacuation. What happened since has been described as the Miracle of Small Ships. Any vessel that could help, small or large, was either requisitioned or went of their own accord and even though the plan called for some 45,000 to be rescued a staggering 338,226 men were recovered. The Calshot RAF base played its part, with boats and seaplanes helping to evacuate British soldiers.

As is always the case during large-scale conflicts, resources were low and much wood was needed. The fast-growing conifers planted in the First World War, along with all those between twenty-five and thirty-five years old were chopped down in one of the largest felling of trees the forest had ever seen. And for the first time since the navy was a wooden flotilla, timber once more returned to the sea to defend our nation – ships, made entirely of wood, were constructed with the sole purpose of being impervious to the German magnetic mine. Once more the British trees of the New Forest played an important role in combat at sea.

Once again, just as during the first war, charcoal burning occurred, with over 40 million gasmask respirators being produced with alder being the wood of choice. Over 5,000 acres were used for bombing ranges, with Ashley Bombing Range (now Ashley Walk) being a test site for the bouncing bomb of dambusters fame. If you take some time to walk along, you can still see the craters from the testing and training that was part of Forest life during the war years. Many of them now serve as watering holes for the New Forest wildlife, oblivious to the fact that so much had ever been at stake. Despite the area's poor fertility, 350 acres of land was requisitioned for agricultural use, to grow crops for the war effort. One such area was at Wiverly Plain, though since the war it has been reseeded and has returned for use as grazing land.

During the war a group was created by Winston Churchill to fight the war through unconventional means, to undertake espionage and sabotage behind enemy lines. This group, going by the name of the Special Operations Executive were partly trained in eleven country homes across the New Forest. Three thousand of the group, also known as the Baker Street Irregulars (after the group in the Sherlock Holmes novels), learnt from professional burglars, librarians, accountants, potters and people from the Intelligence Corps. One such trainer was Kim Philby, who famously defected to Russia in 1963. Their education at Beaulieu was just one part of their training, before they learnt other skills such as demolition and parachuting from other experts around the country – they went on to perform operations all over Europe and became known as Churchill's Secret Army, and the Ministry of Ungentlemanly Warfare. An exhibition focussing on this secret warfare and the role that Beaulieu can be viewed at the Beaulieu Estate (*see* 'Places to Visit').

Much more of the Second World War was fought in the air compared to any previous conflict and again, due to New Forest's southerly location, it made the ideal place for airfields. Nine new airfields were created specifically for the war effort, taking the Forest's total up to twelve. One such airport was RAF Station Stoney Cross, opened in 1942, serving both the RAF and the US Army Air Force (USAAF). Even though it officially opened in November, due to pressures of the war two squadrons had to operate while construction was going on. The airfield was mostly used for bomber and fighter aircraft. Use continued for a few years after the war until it was finally closed in 1948 – the runways were broken up in the 1960s, and the final structure, a water tower, was removed in 2004. However, its marks still remain on the landscape and many and car has unwittingly driven down its main runway, now a minor C road.

Also opened in 1942 was RAF Beaulieu, again used by the RAF and the USAAF, with similar operations running as at Stoney Cross. Even though there had been a small airfield at Beaulieu since 1910, which had been used for flight training during the First World War, it was not deemed suitable and a new airfield was constructed which opened in August 1942. Both this and Stoney Cross were known as class A airfields, with three converging runways, ideally at 60 degrees to each other, allowing take off and landing in any wind conditions, and for all known plane types at the time, including those under construction. In December 1944 the Airborne Forces Experimental Establishment (AFEE) moved to RAF Beaulieu, where they did a lot of work on parachute drops, using the airfield at East Boldre as the drop zone. The AFEE moved to RAF Boscombe Down (near Salisbury) in 1950 and control of RAF Beaulieu changed hands a few times until it was closed in 1959, with the land no longer under military control. Now most of the area has returned to heathland, but a small amount of land is still concreted and is currently used by a Beaulieu model aircraft club. Today Hurn Airport is the only one in the area that is still operating and plays home to Bournemouth International Airport.

Beaulieu seems to have a long-standing relationship with conflict, from the ships built to face the Spanish Armada, to the above airport and once more its riverside location became important. Over 500 craft used the river, many a troop's last ever view of England was the Beaulieu river. Commando units were trained and the area was a large departure point for the D-Day operations, codenamed Operation Overlord.

Lepe is a small town at the mouth of Dark Water. Once a large port, it was destroyed by the great storm in the seventeenth century, but during the war it once more became a site of great importance. Sections of the artificial Mulberry harbours, used to allow quick access of the beaches at Normandy, were partly constructed here before being towed across. The beaches did not naturally lend themselves to such heave usage – so it was deemed necessary for concrete mats to be used on the shingle beaches at Lepe to allow more vehicles to depart for the D-Day invasions.

A not that well-known fact about the invasion of Germany is about how our troops were kept supplied with oil – essential for any modern military. Tankers made easy targets and were also needed elsewhere, yet the delivery of oil was essential. This is where PLUTO came in, Pipe Line Under The Ocean. It was a pipe that went from Lepe, to the Isle of Wight and then under the English Channel all the way to France.

Operation Overlord resulted in the Forest seeing the most action, as troops amassed here ahead of the D-Day invasions and Balmer Lawn Hotel (used as a field hospital in the First World War) was taken over by General Eisenhower and Lord Montgomery as the headquarters for the entire operation. It was from the New Forest that the re-taking of Europe was coordinated.

For more information on the role of the New Forest during the Second World War check out *The New Forest at War* by John Leete.

❀ A NATIONAL PARK ❀

With the New Forest being well past its 900th year it has unsurprisingly seen many changes. The most recent significant change was that it became a National Park in 2005, the culmination of six years' work – but the change into a modern forest began long before that.

Ironically, the modern Forest that you see today has its roots in what was its biggest threat and almost its destruction. In 1871 the Treasury introduced a Bill for the Disafforestation of the New Forest. This had already happened to most of the Royal Forests around the country and would have been disastrous for the New Forest, leaving very little of what we so love today. However, there was such a public outcry that the bill was withdrawn and the New Forest Act of 1877 was passed instead. Not only did this stop the Forest from being destroyed but it also went some way towards recognising the beauty of the Forest and the need for this to be maintained.

It was also through this Act that the Court of the Verderers was re-established, allowing the mingling of old traditions, such as commoners' rights with modern society (*see* 'The Commoners, Their Animals and Forest Law').

In 1923 the Forestry Commission was made responsible for all of the Crown land, some 27,000 hectares, which accounts for 47 per cent of the modern-day National Park.

In 1964 the area got yet another definition of its boundary – the 1964 New Forest Act defined the perambulation of the forest. This is a historic term for the land governed by Forest Law – but in this definition it included all commoners' land, Crown land and privately owned enclosed land – it is the heart of the Forest.

In 1991 it became a Site of Special Scientific Interest (SSSI). This means that the area is of interest for the value of its flora, fauna and geographical features. Under current (post 2000) regulations, any land designated as SSSI is protected from development, damage and neglect.

The next definition to come along was the New Forest Heritage Area, in many ways this was the forerunner to National Park Status. It set up a system of rules relating to planning permission – it is larger than the perambulation but smaller than the National Park. It was identified in 1985, but it was not created until 1992.

In 1993 the Forest was recognised as a Special Protection Area in respect to a number of species of rare bird, particularly the honey buzzard, Montagu's harrier, kingfisher, woodlark, nightjar and the

Parts of the ancient and ornamental woodland date back hundreds of years.

Dartford warbler – of which the Forest now has 75 per cent of the national population. This status requires that the habitats must be maintained and re-established if necessary, as well as taking steps to avoid pollution, disturbances or any other issues that might affect the birds.

It was not until 1999 that work on the National Park began, when they started to look at where the boundaries should lie, and in 2005 it was finally granted National Park Status – one of highest levels of protection that can be conferred by the government, which, along with the other protection statuses, makes it exceptionally difficult to get planning permission to construct anything on New Forest land. Even though it only recently became a National Park, the idea was first proposed at the end of the nineteenth century, after the first one was created in the form of America's Yellowstone National Park in 1872. The status of National Park is an internationally recognised term – to count as one you need a minimum size (1,000 hectares), legal protection by the national government, a budget and staff to provide protection, natural and unaltered ecosystems and, importantly, it must be somewhere that the public have access to.

The New Forest is the smallest National Park in the country at 57,086 hectares, but with 34,000 people living within the boundaries it is also the most densely populated. It has 870 miles of road and some odd place names including Bohemia, Lover and Nomansland.

The sizes of the different areas	Hectares	Square Metres
Crown Land	26,583	107 million
Preamubulation	38,000	153 million
New Forest Heritage Area	53,320	215 million
Naitonal Park	57,086	231 million
New Forest District Council boundary	75,100	304 million

It is estimated that there are 20 million day visits a year to the New Forests and that there were 585,000 camper nights (2004), making the New Forest an important attraction and one that receives a lot of attention – this can be both a good and bad thing. The money brought in by tourism is important to the economic stability and prosperity of the region, with a significant percentage of the population employed in this industry. But this need must be carefully balanced against the conservation requirements of the Forest and the wildlife that inhabits it – some of the laws regarding planning and development may seem restrictive, but they are there to ensure the Forest is around for future generations to enjoy.

The New Forest is a safe haven for many different species and conservation is a key role of all of those bodies that work in the national park – there are overarching conservation programmes and concerns (as outlined above) and there are always smaller, rolling ones, some by the government and some by small charities. One big change imminent is a funding agreement involving Natural England, the verderers, the New Forest National Park Authority, the Forestry Commission and the Commoners Defence Association. This plan, involving everyone who is connected to the New Forest, will see the investment of £16 million over the next ten years – the money will go towards safeguarding all aspects of the Forest. A large part will provide funding for commoning, an activity that has helped to shape the Forest, and its continuation will help it remain unchanged – without the constant grazing of the commoners' animals the heathland and habitats of the New Forest could not survive. It will also help with the restoration of habitats, a big drive for the future of the Forest.

It is good to see that all the key players in the future of the New Forest are taking steps to ensure that it remains what it is today and what it has been for hundreds of years.

Keeping the Forest in check

The New Forest composes a variety of different habitats, from ancient woodland and open heathland to wetland and coastline and it needs constant management and conservation.

Much of the reason for the Forest becoming a National Park concerned conservation, both for the protection of its flora and fauna and to keep it as a place that can be visited and enjoyed. But over the years, as the role of the Forest has changed, different groups have wanted different things. There have been the commoners with their interests and the vereders and agisters who would deal with them; there was the Forestry Commission, originally appointed to ensure there was enough wood for the navy's need; and the keepers, who would look after the animals of the hunt under the order of the Crown. As time has passed, their roles have become less at odds with each other and nowadays they work towards a common goal: a well-managed, healthy forest. But this has not always been the case …

The foresters

The foresters' role, while an old one, does not get much mention in the history books, at least not if you go back much more than 500 years. This is largely due to that fact that when the Forest was created in 1079 it was not considered as a place to grow trees; it was not until much later that this was need, and therefore the need for foresters, became more prominent. Indeed, they were mostly recorded in the annals of history for offences they committed, as opposed to the duties they carried out (*see* 'Corrupt Officials'). It was the keepers, whose job was to safeguard the King's deer, who were mentioned more often (their history and role is outlined in the section below).

It was not until 1438 that the creation of an enclosure for the growing of timber was first recorded; money was paid for 720 perches and 3 gates. In 1535 Godshill Coppice was documented as being a 100-year-old oak plantation. As more and more wood was being used the role of the forester increased, while Royal Hunting in the Forest went into decline. But it was the navy's need for wood that meant the role of the foresters truly became important in the Forest. (*See* 'The Forest at War' for more information on how the New Forest supplied much of the wood needed to keep our shores safe.)

In 1923 the Forestry Commission was set up and made responsible for the management and care of the trees in the Forest. This was a result of the Forestry Act that transferred the New Forest (and the Forest of Dean) to the Ministry of Agriculture. This was done in part to recognise the already present tourism industry that was rapidly increasing.

Their job was extended by the 1949 New Forest Act, which gave them certain responsibilities over the open forest as well, and today they are responsible for the day-to-day management of the entire Forest.

In the open forest (the heathland, which covers roughly 18,000 hectares) the foresters must maintain its traditional character. This entails a programme of controlled burning (to encourage new growth), bracken harvesting, mowing and clearing birches and pines. The burning is important, not just for growth, but to create areas of different aged heather which can help to stop the spread of fire, hence protecting large areas of the forest. This work starts on the first working day of November and ends on the last working day of March. Bracken control takes place in the summer and is done to stop it encroaching on the heather or smothering other plants.

In the ancient and ornamental woodlands little intervention is needed; it consists of mature trees around which animals are free to graze. The only action taken is to remove unwanted foreign plants, the cutting of holly that can otherwise smother others species, and taking into account considerations of tree safety where the public explore.

Timber inclosures still form an important part of the Forest and over 50,000 tonnes of timber are produced each year (*see* 'Tales of Trees and other Plants').

The keepers

The keepers' role is older and different to that of the foresters, but just like the latter the keepers' duties have changed over the years. Originally they had one main aim: to look after the King's deer. A big part of this had been reporting any offences against the deer, but in 1851 their role drastically changed. Instead of looking after the deer they now had to try and kill them, this was down to the Deer Removal Act of 1851. This act was enforced so that more trees could be grown and more timber harvested – grazing deer will harm growing saplings and so the government wanted them removed. However, it was noted that unenclosed pasture land was suffering and due to local pressure the enforcement of this law soon ceased, something that has ensured that the character of the Forest has not changed.

Today their role includes many of the same responsibilities – they still have to look after deer and other animals in the Forest. It is important for the Forest that deer are maintained at a sustainable level – each year the keepers perform a census in April and a shooting plan is then developed. Then during the winter months a cull occurs using high-velocity rifles from specially designed high seats. This is to ensure that the number of deer do not rise above the amount of food available for them. The same happens with other forest animals, such as hares, rabbits and grey squirrels whose numbers must also be kept in check or they will grow to unsustainable levels.

Just like the foresters, the keepers are employed by the Forestry Commission and they can be seen roaming about the Forest, performing a vital task ensuring that the Forest can continue on as it has done for hundreds of years.

The New Forest Park Authority

It is the job of the National Park Authority to ensure that all of these desires and uses of the Forest can mesh and coexist in a sustainable and happy manner. In 2008 they unveiled a controversial new management plan for the Forest, which included dividing the park into zones and even adding toll roads. However, they received over 10,000 responses, and over the following year they revised and changed the plans. The job of a National Park 'is: to conserve and enhance the natural beauty, wildlife and cultural heritage of the National Park; and to promote opportunities for the understanding and the enjoyment of the special qualities of the area by the public.' They also have a duty to foster the economic and social wellbeing of local communities within the National Park. To do this they recognise certain special qualities of the forest:

- The New Forest's outstanding natural beauty
- An extraordinary diversity of plants and animals
- A unique historic, cultural and archaeological heritage
- An historic commoning system
- The iconic New Forest pony
- Tranquillity
- Wonderful opportunities for quiet recreation, learning and discovery
- A healthy environment
- Strong and distinctive local communities

Many people have questioned the need for a management plan, arguing that the Forest has survived for thousands of years without one. But whether or not people have realised it, there has always been a plan of some sorts, even though it may not have been as formal as it is now. Today a plan is certainly needed, with challenges facing the New Forest in every direction, from increased urbanisation and the need for housing, to rising sea levels and climate change and of course the ever-increasing number of visitors.

Whatever changes that will take place over the next ten, twenty or a hundred years, the people of the New Forest will have a say, and thanks to new laws, both domestic and European, it is ensured that the habitat and wildlife of the New Forest will be protected.

two

TALES OF
INTEREST

The New Forest in not just a place where the big history happened. In this section of the book we will explore some of the stories, people and events that make the New Forest such an interesting place. Here you will also find things to do, places to visit and maybe even a nice pub to have a quiet drink in.

❧ THE SNAKE CATCHER ❧

The sun beat down warming his body, it had taken him a while to find this stone, nice and flat, warm from the sun's rays, he was not going to be moving any time soon – no, this was something he was going to enjoy for a while yet. The heat flowed through his body, warming him up in a way that he could not manage, warming up the blood pumping through his body. The forest moved around him as he sat there, basking, his scales soaking up all the warmth that the sun could offer. He twisted, exposing his other side to the sun.

A sound came up from behind him, the snake turned and looked up, his forked tongue snatching at the air. There was a figure standing in front of him, a smell of old clothes and the forest, almost as if the forest and the trees were his clothes. Too late he decided the man was a threat, a tin crashed down on him, scooping him up, trapping him … wriggle and writhe as he might he was trapped, he had no idea where he was being taken, but there was nothing he could do, he was well and truly caught.

One of the best entry points into the New Forest is Brockenhurst railway station. It is one of the largest towns in the Forest and blends the old with the new. You have some traditional village shops but also a large sixth form college – throughout the town, as with the forest, there are cattle grids and gates everywhere, traffic along a busy road will randomly come to a halt as a pony or a donkey decides to take a stroll down the middle of the road.

And of course, it has its fair share of public houses. One such pub, just a couple of minutes walk from the railway station is called the Snakecatcher, named after one Brusher Mills (as of May 2010 the

*The New Forest,
home to many
intriguing stories.*

pub was undergoing a major refurbishment). Harry 'Brusher' Mills was born on 19 March 1840 to a Thomas and Anne Mills and in his sixty-five-year life he managed to become one of the Forest's most eccentric and well-loved figures.

In the mid-1870s Harry became a snake catcher – an obvious choice as snakes were far more abundant in the nineteenth century than they are today. Even as late as 1960 they were considered to be common in the New Forest. A *Times* article of 26 May of that year comments on how, after a study by a Swedish Herpetologist, there were an estimated 25,000 adders in the Forest. So many, in fact, that the Forestry Commission handed out warnings to campers. Hundreds of leaflets were printed, detailing the risks of camping in the Forest and possible snake bites.

In the nineteenth century, unlike today, they were not considered in need of conservation (the whole concept being largely a modern thing), so hunting, capturing and killing them was perfectly legal. If you did it now you would be breaking several laws.

In his lifetime Harry would have caught tens of thousands of snakes from around the Forest, some being sold to London Zoo, some of their skeletons to tourists and others he would have used to make potions and ointments, including his famous remedy for rheumatism, one that he frequently used himself.

In the time before widespread medical treatment, residents of the New Forest would go to Brusher Mills in search of many remedies – an ointment for adder bites could be made from the snake itself. In fact, he was also generally well liked by Forest residents as he removed snakes from their land and he was also well known for his cures for sick animals.

Harry 'Brusher' Mills got his nickname of Brusher from one of his other pastimes – Cricket. He would attend matches at the Balmer Lawn pitch where he would brush the wickets before each and every match.

One of the local legends has it that, in need of a drink, and in no mood to wait for the queue to clear he emptied a bag of snakes onto the floor, parting the crowd like the Red Sea. As to whether he was of a cruel enough disposition for the bag to contain adders is unknown, but the bag would most likely have contained both grass and smooth snakes – the two other species that are found in mainland Britain (*see* 'The Birds and the Bees').

The reason the Snakecatcher public house is called such is not just to honour a popular resident of the forest, it was formerly called the Railway Inn and it was his favourite place to have a quick tipple. It was even in one of the pub's outhouses that he died – he had been living in his hut, near to Sporelake Lawn (where he would often catch snakes) for a considerable time and an old forest law entitled him to claim the land for his own. He was in the process

The Snakecatcher as it stood before its 2010 refurbishment.

Brusher Mills, probably the most famous snake catcher in the country.

of building a more spacious hut when it was destroyed, by vandals, just before completion. It is said that he was left heartbroken, and he died shortly after on 1 July 1905. Those responsible for the destruction of his home were never caught.

After his death, locals paid for a marble tombstone and you can still go and see it in the graveyard at St Nicholas' Church in Brockenhurst. The inscription on the tombstone reads:

This stone marks the grave of
Harry Mills
Better known as "BRUSHER MILLS"
who for a long number of years
Followed the occupation of
Snake Catcher, in the New Forest.

His pursuit and the primitive way
in which he lived, caused him to be
an object of interest to many
He died suddenly July 1st 1905,
aged 65 years

🌸 THE MAGIC OF THE NEW FOREST 🌸

The moonlight filtered through the leaves above them, casting a soft white light on everything. They looked into each others' faces and then to the altar that had been created in the centre of the clearing – it was a simple affair made of wood and stone, quickly but carefully constructed a mere hour ago. They placed some items on it as they chanted under their breaths, speaking phrases, words of powers. They walked around as their chants grew louder, 'Keep her safe, keep her well. Make her safe, make her well.' An owl hooted in the distance as it left its tree, taking to the air and flying towards them. It beat its majestic wings as it circled high into the air, taking a look at the world below it – the alter caught its interest and it swooped down, finding a suitable place to perch. It landed on a branch just above them, observing the proceedings to see if there was anything to eat. One of the witches looked up, her eyes were glazed a perfect white, she looked at the owl, she looked through the owl, and then back to the alter quickly returning her focus to the task at hand.

The owl flew off in search of something more interesting, in search of food, one of the few beings ever to see the coven at work.

'Double, double toil and trouble; Fire burn, and cauldron bubble' – this is the famous chant said by the three witches in Shakespeare's *Macbeth* in Act 4 scene 1 as they put ingredients into the cauldron ready to perform their spells. We have all heard of witches and magic. Whether it is the Wicked Witch in *Sleeping Beauty* or the magic users in *Harry Potter* they are such a common part of modern mythology that you will be hard pushed to find a person who has not come across a story or two.

But witchcraft is not something that is confined simply to the pages of fiction – most places around the country will have some tales about witches or wizards, but none are more apparent than those in the New Forest. It is a place that is renowned for having been the home of several witches and a coven — even if you head down today you will see evidence in Burley of the witchcraft that occurred. How much of this is true, and how much is fabrication has been the subject of much debate.

Wicca is a term that most people would have heard of, with vague associations of magic and a tad of religion, it has been the subject of books and films. But it is something that most people do not know that much about, least of all that a big part of its origin and evolution is based in and around the New Forest.

Wicca is a neo-pagan religion, that is to say it is considered a pagan faith but of modern society, one that has quite possibly taken on aspects of older faiths but has been heavily shaped by modern society, making it a distinct set of beliefs. Wicca is often just refereed to as Witchcraft or the Craft. The word itself is Old English for witch.

Whilst people within Wicca do adopt different theological positions there is a general belief in a god and a goddess, afterlife, morality and, of course, magic. The moral code comes from the Wiccan Rede (meaning advice or council in Old German) — at its most basic it states that you can do what you like so long as you do not harm anybody in the process. There is also the Rule of Threefold Return — either that whatever you do, good or bad, will come back at you three times as strong, or that what you do can affect things on three levels; mental, spiritual and physical. There are eight holy days in the Wiccan Year called Sabbats — including the Equinoxes and Solstices.

A personal book called a book of shadows is kept; this includes spells, potions and other knowledge, and depending on the type of Wicca followed this may or may not be kept secret.

The first time that witchcraft in the New Forest came to the attention of the general public was concerning what has come to be known as the New Forest Coven. They were a group that, or so tales tell, practiced a variety of different magic — one rumour even talks about how, during the Second World War, they emitted a cone of power out across the English Channel to prevent a Nazi invasion of Britain. Seeing that no invasion was forthcoming some have said that they must have been successful, others, of course, are slightly more sceptical.

It was a local man, one Gerald Gardner, a retired civil servant from Christchurch, who told the public about the coven. He said he was initiated into their ranks in 1939 by Dorothy Clutterbuck, better known as Old Dorothy. Such was the public's fascination

Looking for a spell, potion or any other oddities, why not take a look at some of the magic shops in Burley?

that he wrote several books on the subject and became known as 'Britain's Chief Witch' by the BBC – his most famous book was *Witchcraft Today*, published in 1954. The practices that he described here have become known as Gardnerian Wicca.

However, there is a lot of controversy over the New Forest Coven – not over the legitimacy of the magic (which is a whole other issue) but over its very existence. Some claim the whole thing was nothing more than a fabrication by Gardner, a very successful ruse to gain fame. Members of the coven are supposed to have included Edith Woodford-Grimes, Old Dorothy, Rosamund Sabine, Katherine Oldmeadow, Ernie Mason and his sisters Susie Mason and Rosetta Fudge. It is said he met them through the Crotona Fellowship based at a theatre in Christchurch – but the truth of the matter may never be known.

But this was not the last witchcraft that the New Forest saw. The next active practitioner of the art was Sybil Leek, who was dubbed Britain's Most Famous Witch by the BBC. She was born on 22 February in 1917 and she claimed to have come from a family with a long history of witchcraft. She was mostly home taught, only having had three years of normal school education. Her home schooling focussed more on subjects such as herb lore than it did on mathematics. But during her time at home the family would receive visits from people like H.G. Wells and from the famous occultist Alistair Crowley (who formed his own religion and came up with Magik – not a spelling mistake, he really did come up with Magik with a k). At sixteen she married a French pianist but he died two years later, so she was sent by her family to a French Coven. On her return home she stayed for a while in Lyndhurst before spending a year with the Romany gypsies that occupied the New Forest, and it was here where she claims she perfected her knowledge of herbs and their power.

She moved to Burley where she opened up the shop the 'Coven of witches', a shop that is still trading but now under different ownership. She rose to fame after the repeal of the 1735 Witchcraft Act which forbade making any money from this kind of activity – she would have been prosecuted as a vagrant and a con-artist if it had still been in force. But this Act was replaced in 1951 and she quickly rose to fame, having an impact on modern-day Wicca. She wrote over sixty books and in the end became the subject of much attention from the media and tourists – this was not only an annoyance to her but to others in Burley, so much so that she became unpopular and her landlady asked her to move out. This was the end of her relationship with the New Forest and she left for America where she lived out the rest of her life, but her mark on Burley has remained.

It seems that witchcraft is still very much alive in the forest, with white witches still practising their arts – many today are said to be hedge witches, witches that work alone and are not part of a coven.

The actual efficacy of magic is not something that will be gone into here but if you fancy trying it out why not try a love spell to banish that unwanted admirer?

The banishment spell

On a few consecutive days of a waning moon head outside. Using consecrated wood light a fire and throw a handful of vervain leaves while saying out the name of the person you want removed from your life, then chant the following words:

> I need you not.
> I want you not.
> Leave my life now
> And come back never.
> And it harm none, so be it.

Think about the person's face in the fire … you should see it disappear from your life … or at least that is what is supposed to happen!

❧ A SMUGGLER'S HAVEN ❧

> *He hated doing this in the day, the night was his friend, he would wear the cloak like darkness, it would keep him hidden, it would keep him safe. But the sun? No, that wasn't his friend at all. It lit up the world and him along with it. Him and the spices that he was smuggling in. Still, he thought, trying to relax, he wasn't about to get caught around here. The forest offered him ample protection, even if the sun wanted to point him out the trees would keep him hidden. And besides … there was always a way to know if the authorities were around. A short walk, with his goods stashed in a safe spot, took him into view of Vereley Hill. She wasn't there … simultaneously he was pleased and saddened – the fact that she wasn't there meant that he was safe, that his goods were safe. She only came out, dressed in brilliant red, when the Riding Officer, out to arrest him, was around. The only down side was that a part of him wanted her to be there, just for a glimpse.*
>
> *Returning to his goods he had a quick check that they were still there, then he made his way to the meeting point. The coaches would be there soon, they would load the goods, and after that it wouldn't be long until the money started coming in. He smiled, it was a good day, it was a smuggler's life.*

With so many beaches, ravines, chines and of course the woodland itself, the New Forest offered an ideal location for smuggling and smugglers. To this very day evidence of their illegal escapades can still be seen throughout the Forest.

In the eighteenth and nineteenth centuries smuggling stopped being a small scale occurrence and turned into what was almost an industry – some accounts even claim that the tea for four out of every five cups drank in England had been smuggled in, and that most people, in some way, were involved in the activity. Be it as a smuggler, distributor or end-user, the majority of people were connected to this illegal importing of goods.

The main reason for such a large social participation in smuggling was the very high taxes imposed on the British population, in part to pay for the government to wage war overseas. During this time these taxes were split into two types – customs and excise, a term that is still around today. Customs dealt with imports, and had been going on for many hundreds of years. The Crown had claimed a percentage of all cargoes coming into the country, either physically, or in monetary equivalent. Excise, however, was new to the time, a tax on produce consumed within the country; it covered chocolate, coffee, tea, alcohol and other things such as salt, leather and soap. The high taxation, sometimes as much as half the value you were paying for tea, was hard on an already poor population, many of whom were already close to starving. Their answer was smuggling; better known to locals as Free Trade.

Smugglers would, often under the cover of darkness, head across the English Channel with goods that they had purchased in Europe. Many would then make their way to the New Forest, and use the distribution network that had been set in place to get the goods sold, making money for themselves and giving locals what they needed – cheaper goods. Said goods included tea, alcohol of all sorts, spices, silks and even the occasional aristocrat fleeing the French revolution.

One such place used by smugglers, for meeting, planning and storage, was the Queen's Head Pub, a sixteenth-century pub in the village of Beaulieu. Indeed it was notorious for both smugglers and highwaymen and in recent refurbishments a hidden cellar was discovered under the floorboards. What was discovered beneath the floor where the stable had once been was a veritable stash, including pistols, bottles and coins.

Of course though, the law was not just going to sit idly by and let those dastardly scoundrels break the rules of the land and evade taxes, unjust ones or otherwise. Stopping the smugglers was down to the The Riding Officer of Customs and Excise and the few men under his command – they were neither popular with the smugglers or the general population. Those smuggling would be on the constant lookout for these officers, and one family in Beualieu offered a helping hand in this matter.

The Warne family, living in a house called Knaves Ash at Crow Hill Top were all involved in one way or another with smuggling. There was John, Peter and Lovey – and it was Lovey who had the job of warning those partaking of free trade that the Riding Officer was around. She would climb Vereley Hill wearing a bright red cloak, all in the surrounding areas could see her and they knew this meant that the Riding Officer was in the forest and that it was time to lie low, hide the stash and act innocently. Tales also tell of how she used to take a more active roll in smuggling, boarding a ship in Christchurch harbour, undressing in the captain's cabin where she would then warp herself in fine silks, putting her clothes back on and then walking out and home as if nothing was amiss – though as folklore would have us believe this all came to an end when one of the officers asked her for a drink at the Eight Bells, a public house in Christchurch, and got a little friendly and hands on, his hands finding more than they bargained for.

Punishments for smugglers were not lenient, with both transportation and death being possibilities – by the roadside at Mark Way there are the remains of a tree in the middle of some heath surrounded by a fence – the tree used to be known as the Naked Man – an infamous spot where the hangman put his skills into practice.

Smugglers hid things wherever they could, with two common sayings being, 'Keystone under the hearth,' and 'keystone under the horse's belly,' referring, respectively, to a stash in a safe place under a burning home fire, and under the stables. There are still rumours that there are hidden cashes in the Forest under thick cover of bracken that have been left untouched for hundreds of years. Maybe if you are lucky enough you will stumble upon some hidden treasure …

🌸 GHOSTLY GOINGS ON 🌸

The building was old; it had an old feel to it, almost as if it had never been new. It had probably felt old the day it had been built. It got a lot of use though, people came and went, it was a nice little pub to have a sit down in and a nice, quiet drink. It was somewhere for a weary traveller to rest his legs after a long day walking in the forest. He picked up his cider from the table, taking a long, slow sip, feeling the bubbles play along his tongue and course down his throat. It was his second pint and he was going to enjoy it, it had been a long day and he deserved a nice drink. He caught a glimpse of white reflecting in the glass, he turned his head to see what had disturbed his drinking, and there she was, just for a moment, or so he would swear years later; a woman, all in white, from her head to her toes, her hair, her face, her shoes, her very skin, she was all white. He looked at her, it couldn't have been for long, no more than a second, and then she disappeared into nothing, or at least, so he would say.

The New Forest is no stranger to the odd ghost story, many have probably been told outside a tent late at night, as the wind howls through the trees and people try to scare each other. But there are a few a little more convicing than the average fireside tale that you will hear.

Murder and mystery

An Elizabethan manor house in Breamore, unimaginatively named Breamore House, near Fordingbridge, is home to the Hulse family, who took over the estate in the eighteenth century, when the then physician to King George I bought the property. Today Breamore House holds many fine works of art and exquisite pieces of furniture. But it is said that the previous occupants, those that had commissioned the construction, never quite left the property. Built in 1853 for the Dodington family, it was their home for hundreds of years – if you are unlucky enough to find yourself alone, or take a wrong turn, you may find yourself face to face with one of their ghosts. One of the Dodginton Ladies so admired her portrait that, on her death bed she put a curse on anyone who would move it … nothing was thought of it until the 1950s when a cleaner moved the painting and hours later suffered a fall and broke his leg. No one has dared move it since. The other Dodington was murdered in a fit of rage by her son in the blue bedroom, which she now haunts; she is said to appear whenever there is serious illness or death.

Whilst in the area, a great place to visit is the mizmaze in Breamore. It is one of only eight surviving ancient turf mazes in the British Isles. The word 'maze' is slightly misleading in several senses. There are no tall bushes, no diverging paths and no directions to chose. You can see the whole of the maze before you start your journey around it – the pattern is cut into the grass, not grown using bushes. The point is not to hide the maze from your view, indeed the purpose of these turf mazes in not known for certain. Some suggest they were for entertainment whilst others say that they were created as a form of religious penance where someone in need of redemption would have to walk around on their hands and knees. Two of these eight turf mazes are referred to as mizmazes and are not even a maze as one would traditionally think of as a puzzle on a piece of paper – there are no branches or stems, it is just one long route that you follow from start to finish, following the grass path until you reach the centre. It is not known how old many of them are, as due to constant re-cutting, archaeological evidence is often disturbed or destroyed.

Not far from the start of the mizmaze in Breamore's Churchyard is a yew tree under which three stone coffins are buried. And you may even encounter a pair of ethereal monks standing by the tree, floating their way towards the mizmaze, perhaps as penance for some wrongdoing they did centuries before.

The Rufus Stone is an attraction in its own right, marking the supposed spot where King William Rufus was shot dead by a stray arrow in 1100 (see 'Death in the Forest'). The circumstances surrounding his death will most likely always remain a mystery with numerous theories abounding – one such theory is that Walter Tyrrell, either killing the King by accident, or believing he would receive the blame, fled to his lands in Normandy. On route his escape took him down what is now known as a Tyrrell's Lane in Burley – on a summer's evening you could encounter them both, William Rufus next to the monument marking his death, and Sir Walter Tyrrell on his path to freedom. If you visit the area on the anniversary of Rufus' death you may come across a pond glinting red in the moonlight – Ocknell Pond, two miles away from the Rufus Stone, was a supposed stopping point on Tyrrell's flee from the Forest, and each year the pond is said to no longer be filled with water, but flowing red with blood.

Haunted pubs

Everyone likes a good drink, and according to locals the enjoyment of a good beer is not just something confined to the living.

As detailed in the section on smuggling, the Queen's Head pub in Burley has been used extensively for plotting, storing and for general activities in the day-to-day life of a smuggler. From the late 1800s onwards moaning could often be heard from beneath the bar, and it was not until the renovations in the 1950s, that revealed the hidden den, that this stopped. Perhaps it was just old floorboards under stress, or maybe, as some would claim, it was the spirit of smugglers who wanted their goods to reach their final destination, not to spend an eternity just metres away from their intended audience.

An odd thing may strike you about the Tudor Rose Inn of Burgate, near Fordingbridge. You will notice an odd lack of doors – this is because the current landlady has removed any doors that were not needed. It all began in 1967 when the owners of the fourteenth-century inn started to hear footsteps on and around the stairs, with staff claiming to see the shape of a woman drifting along the corridors upstairs. The Paraphysical Laboratory of Gloucester investigated these reports, but to no avail. It did not stop here though … in what is perhaps a separate haunting a figure would knock on a door before entering a room, slamming the door behind them – this is claimed to be the ghost of a cavalier. It is for this reason that the landlady removed as many doors as she could.

Locals claim that the Angel, an eighteenth-century coaching inn located in the picturesque town of Lymington, is home to no less than four ghosts. One is an old coachman who looks in at the customers, with his nose pushed up against the window, while another regales them with his playing of an absent piano. The third is a little girl who skips along merrily on the second floor whilst there is also a sailor in a reefer jacket who also frequents the inn.

At the White Heart in Ringwood staff claim that there is a door that will not stay open, regardless of what is used to prop it up, and that the ghost responsible is a chambermaid who is obsessed with neatness, even apparently tidying up after people. Despite this helpful tendency an exorcism was carried out in the 1960s, with the cross carved into the wall by the stairs still visible to anyone who cares to take a look.

Another inn, the Bluebeckers White Hart near Candam, is also said to be haunted. The smell of expensive perfume fills the inn as you enter, followed by the sound of swishing silk and a drop in temperature – no one knows who this lady might have been.

Hangings were no uncommon thing, especially where highway men were concerned and one such place of execution was at Marlpit Oak, where a gibbet stood. Three men were hanged and buried there and, according to local legend, from the Hare and Hounds Inn you can see three ghosts making their way across the car park to the point where their lives were abruptly ended.

The Wagon and Horses pub in Walhampton in Lymington gains its notoriety from a tragic accident that occurred there in 1893. A farmer was found shot in the back with his own shotgun. There seemed to be no motive or suspects in his death yet people were dubious that anyone could shoot themselves in the back with their own shotgun. The local gamekeeper, Henry Card, went on to show people how such an accident could occur, if the gun was held in the right way, and the right actions were taken … sadly though he did not think to unload his gun and he died in the same way as the poor farmer. Since then, his presence has been noted at the bar of the Wagon and Horses.

Abbey apparitions

Beaulieu Abbey is considered to be one of the most haunted places in Britain. Its history is a long one, almost as long as the Forest's. It was founded by King John in 1204. It was the first Cistercian abbey in England and was occupied by thirty monks from the French Abbey of Cîteaux, the home of the Cistercian Order (in Latin the name of the abbey is actually *Bellus Locus Regis*, meaning the Beautiful Place of the King). Much damage was done during the Dissolution of the Monasteries by Henry VIII but it is still a beautiful place, drawing in many visitors each year, some of which undoubtedly come in the hope of seeing some of the abbey's ghosts.

The first recorded instance of haunting occurred between 1886 and 1939 when the vicar of Beaulieu often encountered the ghosts – he claimed to know all of their names and included them as part of his congregation, even remarking to someone attending his service that it had been well attended, not empty as it may have seemed to the untrained eye.

The smell of incense is often noted, coming unaccounted for from an upstairs room that had previously been used as a chapel. A grey lady is also seen walking the halls; visitors have often asked why the grey-clad, costumed guide, would not talk to them. She is thought to be Isabella, Countess of Beaulieu, who died in 1786. An age-old funeral has also been played out, with it being heard near to the monks' burial grounds, where the sound of a spade in earth can be clearly discerned.

So many reports were made of hauntings in the abbey that the Living TV show, *Most Haunted*, did an episode on the abbey which aired on 31 October 2003.

A strange photograph

Just north of the village of Fritham, near Lyndhurst, lies Eyeworth pond. One day, during a hunt, a photograph was taken of the lake and clearly visible in the background was a lady wearing clothes from another era. The photograph has been proved to be genuine yet no one has been able to identify this mysterious apparition who has so captured people's imaginations.

Nothing above the neck

Lady Alice Lisle was born in 1617 and lived in turbulent times. In 1685 Lord Monmouth led a rebellion against King James II, the elder brother of the now dead Charles II. James' ascension was unpopular with many due to his Roman Catholic faith. Lord

Monmouth, however, was an illegitimate son of Charles II, and the rightful heir, or so he felt. The rebellion culminated on 6 July 1685 at the Battle of Sedgemoor. With the rebellion over, Monmouth's supporters fled, going into hiding wherever they could. Two such supporters, John Hicks and Richard Nelthorpe, sought shelter at Lady Lisle's residence of Moyles Court, near Ringwood. After just one night at her abode, 20 July 1685, they were arrested, as was she for harbouring traitors. At the age of sixty-nine she was put on trial for treason. Despite asserting that she had not know from what they were hiding, she was found guilty, albeit reluctantly, and sentenced to burning that afternoon. The sentence though was commuted by James II to beheading which was carried out in Winchester Market Place on 2 September 1685.

Today her sentencing is considered unfair, even judicial murder by some, and perhaps it is for this reason that even to this day she has been seen walking around Moyles Court with her head under her arm along with a coach drawn by headless horses … supposedly if you can smell violets in the air she is not too far away.

A creepy construction

One of the most well known things about the small town of Sway, and certainly the most noticeable, is the striking Sway Tower that stands at 218ft tall. It is also known as Peterson's Folly after the man who had it built on his land. Judge Andrew Thomas Peterson had it constructed between 1879 to 1885. It is made of unreinforced concrete with the only iron being around the windows. This makes it a World Record holder – it is the tallest non-reinforced concrete structure in the world.

It is said that the construction was influenced by his involvement with a medium – the medium contacted the spirit of Sir Christopher Wren who gave them the plans, perhaps explaining its original intended usage as a mausoleum. A permanent light was meant for the top, but it was not allowed for fears of confusing local shipping. Today it is a Grade II listed building and is a privately owned bed and breakfast.

❧ THE LIFE OF A TRAVELLER ❧

It was a long way to go, they all knew that, but something like this didn't happen every day. It was odd to be travelling back to the New Forest after so many years. It had been, what, twenty years? The last time he had been there was when he was a child – he still remembered the pony they had bought from him, a fowl, a young New Forest Pony. Of course, that is why they were going back, the three of them, because of him. Because he had died. Normally they would not travel the entire length of the country for a funeral, they would show their respects from wherever they might be – but news had reached them, news had reached everyone. He had been a friend, he had almost been a father – their life consisted of travelling anyway, so they may as well travel back down to the Forest.

The sun glinted off their caravan as the pony, the child of the one they had been given all those years ago, pulled them along, as they made their way down south. Passers by would admire the caravan, the bright colours, but they were all hoping it would not be stopping. No one liked them. Except for other gypsies.

It would take them three days to make their way down. It would be good to meet up with everyone, and it would be good to say goodbye. It had been too long. Undoubtedly he would be the one to stay up with the body the night before it was buried, they would wait for him, they had, after all, called for him specially.

Most people will have come across the term 'gypsy', with various connotations being attached to the word, but they have had a long relationship with the forest that has lasted hundreds of years.

Both the term 'gypsy' and 'traveller' are used to describe Romany people. The first record of gypsies in England dates from the fifteenth-century and this is when the word also first appeared. It was originally believed that they had originated from Egypt, with the word gypsy being a corruption of this – but recent research has shown that they originally came from medieval India.

Their presence in the New Forest was first noted in the Chawton's parish records for 1638 – but by this time several laws had already been passed to deal with the presence of these travellers. Gypsies were not very welcome in England or the New Forest – in 1530 the Egyptians Act was passed in attempt to remove all of the gypsies from England – it banned immigration and all gypsies already in England had to leave within sixteen days. In 1554 this was changed, imposing the death penalty for any who did not leave within one month. Even though a second Egyptian Act in 1783 repealed these previous laws the regulations passed still impacted heavily on their lives, and even today laws and public opinions are not entirely welcoming.

A good example of the antipathy towards gypsies over the years can be seen from an article in the the *Times* from Monday, 29 December 1949. The article starts with the line, 'The New Forest gypsies have never had many friends; today they have still fewer.' It goes on to talk about how the New Forest committee condemned them and their way of life and that villages near the camps, 'suffer something more than inconvenience from these undesirable neighbours.' One compound in particular was talked about, Shave Green with a total population of about 130 people, unwelcome and unliked by the locals; even those that had served in the army during the Second World War, and had taken up paid work with the Forestry Commission were still not liked – the article ends by stating that those who lived in the New Forest said, 'the simple solution is to remove all the gypsies as soon as possible to some place at least five miles distant from the perambulation of the Forest.'

When all is said and done, most of the general population do not know much about gypsies and their way of life, but their influence on English culture has been noticeable. For example, the word 'pal', something that is in common parlance today, is originally a Romany word meaning brother. Their identity, colourful clothes and large jewellery have become part of common knowledge, with parts of their culture being instantly recognisable – but if you ask someone what it actually means to be Romany, or to describe their culture, then most people would be at a loss – even though there was no small presence of gypsies in the Forest, with Sybil Leek, a white witch, supposedly learning vast amounts of herb lore from them (*see* 'The Magic of the New Forest') while Harry 'Brusher' Mills, or so the tales go, did not get along with them at all (*see* 'The Snake Catcher').

What follows is by no means a comprehensive description of their customs, it is simply an introduction and a little bit of information to help you know them a little better.

Probably the most prevailing image of the Romany people within the minds of most of the population is their method of travel, their caravans. Of course this is not the modern-day image that you have of a caravan, towed behind a truck and so detested by other car users – these were the more traditional horse-drawn kind.

Painted in bright colours, they would be the home of the travelling gypsy, if not the actual sleeping place; often, and particularly in the New Forest, they would sleep in what they would called benders, a type of tent so named due to its method of construction – a branch, usually beech, would be bent into an arch with a sheet of tarpaulin thrown over it creating an instant domicile.

The horse-drawn caravan, also known as a vardo, was only used for around 100 years during the nineteenth and twentieth centuries, yet their image is the most enduring of those associated with gypsies (before then small carts were used with travel by foot not being uncommon). There is one such caravan, recently restored, that it is located in Sandy Balls Wood at Godshill. The story goes that a young gypsy man fell madly in love with a young gypsy woman, but before she would consent to be his wife he would have to have a caravan that would be the pride of any gypsy bride. So he went about making the finest caravan, with bright colours and intricate designs – but, before they could live happily ever after, she died, leaving him bereaved and alone. Perhaps it was then that he carved their faces at the corners of the door lintel, so that no one would ever forget that it was made for two gypsy lovers.

Travelling in their caravans was a central part of their culture. They would travel in small family groups, usually one caravan alone, but sometimes as many as three. Moving around the country would allow them to visit other gypsies at regular stopping points (known as atchin tan) – grassy lanes would be favourite spots, something the New Forest was ideal for. Meetings with others would be common, with children taking a central place whilst elders were greatly respected. Traditionally though, children would not receive much in the way of formal education. Most often the boys would be taught skills and crafts by their fathers whilst the girls would be taught housekeeping skills by their mothers. Today, of course, things are slightly different; in the 1970s a special education programme was set up in the UK and there are around 200 specially trained teachers, with around one third of travellers' children attending school regularly. If a site is set up for travellers, of any kind, the local council will make an assessment of all children on site.

Cleanliness is extremely important amongst a gypsy family – any animals owned, including dogs, are not allowed within the caravan or near any kitchen utensils or food items. Things that are unclean are known as mokadi and mahrime, customs and guidelines that have been learnt from travelling on the road for hundreds of years. The group of unclean items would also include women when they were giving birth, which traditionally would have been done in a birthing tent, away from any men, and the fathers would not touch the baby until it had been christened. Today it is normal practice for the birth to take place in hospital with the fathers attending. But of course before the birth marriage would normally occur; despite their travelling nature the ceremony would usually be done in a traditional church – often marriages would be between different gypsy families though it was not, and still is not, uncommon for gorgers (non-gypsies) to be married.

Where death is concerned the rituals are slightly more interesting. When a traveller died a vigil would be held. The body would not be left alone or in the dark until the burial, often with several people sitting with the body lest a ghost would be brave enough to approach a lonely observer. The dead would be buried with valuable possessions and their other worldly belongings would be burnt, not being passed on (some say in case the souls of the dead come back to claim what is theirs). It is not unusual for gypsies to travel a long way to attend the funeral for another, some drawing large crowds.

One of the things that made the New Forest attractive for gypsies was the seasonal work that could be found in the surrounding area. This would mostly be harvesting crops such as hops and strawberries, and the labour they brought was invaluable to the economic growth of the area. But as modern machinery was brought in during the 1930s this work became scarce and the work that was done shifted to other trades, with things such as scrap metal dealing and building trades such as roofing becoming more common.

Today many gypsies live in normal accommodation or at permanent sites, working in any career sector, but their traditions and heritage are no less important today than when they were when they first entered the forest some 500 years ago.

🌺 MOVERS AND SHAKERS 🌺

It would be on a day like this, wouldn't it? The clouds were showing them no mercy as the full force of the weather fell down upon them in earth shattering droplets. None of the hundred and sixty among them had managed to stay dry – but still, they thought, God would provide for them, God would protect them. They had to, after all, survive to the second coming, one that clearly had not yet come.

> They lined the road, along with everything that the community had ever owned, beds were strewn along the grass, farming equipment littered the verges. The people would dry out without a problem, but all of their stuff, furniture, food, even pianos, might not be so lucky.
>
> It had all started months ago, all over something as petty as money. Money they owed people, money they thought that was not a problem. Why did these people want them out? What had they done? They had led a blameless existence here, people may have not shared their beliefs, but they had never hurt anyone. They had never come close.
>
> A crowd, of sorts, had been drawn. Some people had just come to watch, some with sympathy and some with glee. Those that felt sorry had taken some of their possessions to store them from the worst of the weather, there had even been a couple of offers of shelter for them, but their leader had been sure of her convictions. God would provide.

In a rather odd tale a religious community in the New Forest was the centre of scrutiny, eviction and sympathy all within a short space of time.

It all started some 150 years ago when Mary Ann Girling, daughter of a Suffolk farmer, celebrated Christmas in 1858. Upon this day she claimed that Christ appeared to her with a simple message. In contemporary interviews she stated that, 'Am I reasonable now? Do I seem calm and undisturbed, speaking to you? Then just as calmly, with just as little disturbance of mind and judgement did I see the face of the Most High, and receive the blessed assurance that this weak body of mine should not see death.' So it was that she would lead the Children of God to the promised land during the Second Coming, which, according to her, was nigh as she went on to say, 'It was vouchsafed to me to see a face as distinctly as your own – to hear a voice telling me plainly that I should live to see the Second Advent.'

From here she tried to fulfil what she had claimed to see in her vision and quickly set up a commune in London. However, this was not really suitable to the lifestyle that she felt God wanted them to lead. Part of this was tilling the land and growing their own food, and for this they needed their own space. Thankfully, one of the members, the aptly named Miss Julia Woods, was in possession of a sum of money, and put £3,000 to purchasing some land in the New Forest and they purchased the New Forest Lodge, in Hordle.

The thirty-one-acre Lodge, costing £4,000 in total, required a mortgage of £1,000 to be taken out. It was this secured loan that would cause them so much grief in the future.

But even before their money troubles began they had already gained a reputation with the people in the local community. It was their religious beliefs that set them most apart from other inhabitants of the New Forest – not only did they all believe that Mrs Girling was a prophet but they all felt themselves to be immortal, that no harm could come to them until the second coming. Some people felt that the whole thing was little more than a cult, with parents sometimes turning up demanding that their sons or daughters returned. Whilst their beliefs were very similar to that of the American Shakers, with no strong liquor, a separation of the sexes and a lot of worship thorough joyful singing and dancing, they did not consider themselves such. Mrs Girling called the group Bible Christians, as this was the only book they followed, in fact it was the one and only book that she had ever read. She gained a reasonable following; at its height there were over 160 members.

A lot of people though were not nearly as happy; at one point she was even branded as a witch and was threatened with being burnt. In the end, however, it was not her arrest that led to the community in the New Forest having to move on; instead it was the simple matter of a missed mortgage payment. It was in 1873 when they first defaulted, missing an interest payment of the sum of £25. By the time it came for collection to be enforced this had risen, including fines, up to £40. Far more than this was taken – two horse and two cows. The horses alone were valued at £130, but despite this the lot was sold for £130, with the group not seeing any of the difference. They did not even ask for it, just assuming it would be put towards the next mortgage payment, choosing instead to simply trust the law enforcement officers who had been responsible for collection of the debt. However they defaulted a second time, hit hard by the loss of their livestock. This time though there was little left to take and no one to come to their aid – even though they were given three months to pay they could not do so, and then, after they failed to make good the debt, they were given twelve days to vacate the land. They still did not do, simply thinking that God would come to their aid. But God did not provide and they were moved, in the pouring rain, onto the road along with all of their possessions. The estate was sold for the much smaller sum of £1,340 – this however, is not as low as it may sound, as much of the work they had done, such as the conversion of an agricultural barn into a chapel, would have to be undone. Yet again they did not see all of the difference, only receiving the measly sum of £70 – no one is entirely sure where the difference ended up, but most likely in an official's pocket.

They remained in the road, in the harsh weather, until 9 p.m. that evening when finally they were offered, and accepted, the shelter of a barn. They stayed there for a couple of weeks until they set up home in Tiptoe, near Lymington. Here they rented a farm, setting up tents and other ramshackle accommodation.

Their plea, and harsh treatment by the authorities, brought them much attention in the UK and from farther afield, with an article even being published in the *New York Times* in 1875. The article was not flattering, referring to Mrs Girling's 'deluded followers,' and stating that the appeal for funds was unfounded, as some of the people making it were in possession of more than enough jewellery and other finery that could have well sustained them.

The group survived at Tiptoe until 1886, when the supposedly immortal Mrs Girling died of cancer. She was buried in Hordle churchyard with eleven of her disciples, with nothing but a cypress tree marking the spot. The controversy surrounding her did not end with this though, as more recently arguments ensued over whether a new parish hall should be built on the land, with many different groups of people speaking out against it – but a ruling was passed and permission for the hall was given – whether any more is to be heard from or about the prophet only time will tell.

❧ CORRUPT OFFICIALS ❧

He looked around, things clearly were not how they were meant to be, the man had enclosed a good acre more land than he should have.

'You've got yourself into a bit of trouble here,' he said, looking over the land.

'It's only a little bit over.'

'You know the law is strict on this.'

The two men paused, looking at each other. They both knew where this was heading, but neither of them wanted to make the first move, just in case they had misread the situation.

But the rumours had been going around, the owner knew about this man, he had been told it would not take much.

> 'Your planning permission says you should have the fence ten metres closer to your house.'
> The man looked around again, the owner knew that this was his cue.
> 'Nothing we can do about it?' he said as he handed over an envelope, a full envelope.
> 'You know,' he said, as if thinking things over, 'I don't think it's that much of a big deal to be honest, I'm sure it's just a clerical error.'

No matter where you are, certain people in power will always take advantage of their positions of authority and the New Forest was no exception to this, with many an official finding themselves at the wrong end of the law. By and large the people that work in and around the Forest are hard working and honest, with the best interests of the Forest at heart, but below are detailed a few of the people who had a slightly different world view.

One of the more common and frequent misuses of power was by the officials who were supposed to 'law dogs'. This was the process of laming any dog large enough to worry deer – but quite often a bribe would be enough to stop this.

Dogs were often lamed to prevent them from worrying the Forest deer.

In the early days of the Forest it was the keepers, not the foresters, who had the most important and prominent role, in fact it was to

such an extent that the most evidence of foresters is actually from their misdeeds, not their lawful actions. One such forester to break the law was Walter de Kanc, who was investigated in 1271, when it was reported that he had taken one hart and six bucks (male of the red and fallow deer respectively). The other foresters and verderers had not only known about these deer, but they admitted to also knowing that he had taken around 500 deer during his time in office – a staggering number. The Foresters and Verderers were reprimanded but the serious punishment was reserved for Walter de Kanc, the man who had been stealing the deer – and such was the custom at the time, the punishment was severe (*see* 'Commoners, Their Animals and Forest Law'). He was fined £5,000, a veritable fortune by today's standards and he and his family were placed at the will of the King and the Queen – this meant that he was their property, the Royal Family could do whatever they so chose with the Kanc family.

I   Small and cute, the Shetland
pony is far more distinctive than
its New Forest cousin.

2 The New Forest pony will pretty much eat anything.

3 Wild boar, something that has not been seen Wild in the Forest for many a year.

4 & 5 *The easiest deer to spot in the Forest the fallow deer are easily identifiable.*

6, 7 & 8 Red deer are a herd animal, if you
are lucky enough to come across one they will
likely stop for a few moments to look at you,
just as you look at them.

9, 10, 11 & 12 The New Forest is home to numerous species of small bird, both rare and common.

13 The common blue tit.

14 The swan is no stranger to the Forest …

15 ... nor are mallards.

16 Birds of prey are common, with Kestrels being the easiest to spot over open land.

17 One of the owl species that can be
found in the Forest is the long-eared owl.
They can be very hard to spot. They are
usually silent and only active at night.

18 Watch where you step,
lest you tread on an adder …

19 … or a grass snake,
the UK's largest reptile.

20 & 21 *The New Forest is an important habitat for many different species of butterflies and moth.*

22 The British bumble bee is still very common within the New Forest and it plays an invaluable role in pollinating plants, ensuring that the area continues to flourish.

23 Hard to spot, shieldbugs are common over the forest and often quite well camouflaged.

24 The broad bodied chaser.

25 The golden ringed dragonfly.

26 Bright yellow, sharp and smelling of coconut gorse bushes can be seen all over the forest.

27 The paper bellflower.

28 & 29 The rich and diverse plant and flower life in the New Forest is not only nice to look at but plays an important role in the ecosystem of the forest. Numerous different flowers can be seen in the Forest, both those that are native to the UK and those that have been introduced (such as the purple bellflower picture above).

three

MODERN LEGENDS

We have taken a look back at interesting events that have occurred over the last 1,000 years. Some are rooted firmly in fact, such as the Norman invasion and the latter creation of the Forest. Some are true but surrounded in mystery, such as the suspicious death of William Rufus. Others are mere folklore with no basis in anything other than superstition, such as Brusher Mills' cure for rheumatism, or the witches in Burley.

In 100, 200, or even 1,000 years what will be remembered of today? In this section we will take a look at some of the more interesting or bizarre occurrences that have taken place within the New Forest over the last decade. As to what will be talked about in a millennia from now, your guess is as good as mine.

🌺 POWERFUL PIGS 🌺

Pigs have always played a vital role in the forest by clearing the ground of the numerous acorns in the autumn and thus preventing potentially lethal consumption by other New Forest animals – but it appears that they have been playing a more interesting role here and there as well.

And they're off ...
We have all heard of horses and greyhound racing, but I wonder how many of you have been to a pig race? In Damerham this is just what they do – race pigs. The pigs are trained for one month, reaching a weight of 35kg, to take part in the town's very own pig race. Forty pigs take part and money is usually raised for charity, in 2009 it was to raise money for a local sports field. But possibly the oddest thing about the race of 2009 was the fact that it was hosted by Murry Walker, more famous for his Formula One commentary rather than his porcine knowledge.

Hungry little pigs
Even the pig's mundane ability to eat has given us two interesting little tales – the first was as a replacement to pesticides. Pigs may not seem a natural substitute to chemicals but this is just how they have been used in a couple of areas. In places that have been

Clearly an animal bred for speed and manoeuvrability!

particularly affected by the weed Gaullerie (better known as American Strawberry), nuts would be scattered on the ground, the dutiful pigs would then root around finding them, digging up the weed. This process breaks up the root of the plant, stopping its spread which is just as well, as it grows so thick and dense that it stops other plants from growing at all.

The second instance of their incredible and useful gluttony goes back to the autumn tradition of eating acorns in the forest. Except of course it is more than just a tradition – in 1968 eighty ponies and forty cattle died from digesting lethal amounts of them. The pig's role is essential – yet in 2006 there was such a large shortage of pigs that the Forestry Commission had to ask for more of them to be turned out – an extra 300 in total. Seeing as only commoners are allowed to do this that is a lot of extra pigs!

Chasing pigs ...

In 2006 a police officer was out with his dog, patrolling the usually tranquil New Forest. Spotting a patch of pink in the distance the officer decided it would be a good opportunity to familiarise his dog with the animals that he had yet to encounter. The pig ran off – but not to retreat, he came storming back with over ten of his friends, chasing the dog and the policeman back to their vehicle. Locking themselves safely away in the police car they thought they were safe and the matter was closed. Unfortunately, as if this were not embarrassing enough, the whole affair had been recorded on someone's mobile phone and it was up on Youtube that evening for people to watch.

🌺 DUTIFUL DOGS 🌺

In the 2003 Golden Bonio awards, a prize set up to award our extraordinary canine friends, a dog from the New Forest, a two-year-old labrador, made it to the twelve finalists.

On a day out at sea with his owner, he fell overboard just one mile from the coast of the Isle of Wight. Normally, claimed the owner, the dog would be wearing a life jacket, but due to the warm weather the dog had not been wearing one when he went overboard. Four hours of searching by the owner sadly revealed nothing and he thought that his pet was lost forever. But Todd the labrador did not give up the game, nor did he swim the one mile to the nearest landfall – no, instead of taking the easy route and despite being out at sea he made for home. Heading out across the busy shipping lane of the Solent he swam ten miles, not even content to stop at the coast he continued up the Beaulieu River until he finally came ashore. Here he was found by a boy who took him to a local police station. Thankfully, the dog had been micro-chipped and could be returned home to his owner in the New Forest.

Sadly Todd did not win the prize, which went to a Siberian Husky named Rio who encouraged his anorexic owner back to health. Other finalists included Bertie, a hearing aid dog, who was visiting his owner in hospital when he noticed the woman in the bed next to him had stopped breathing, and alerted the nurses; Bobbie, a male greyhound who adopted seven puppies; a police dog who was stabbed while protecting a policeman; and a guide dog who was attacked by another dog, but still took his owner home and upstairs before passing out – the dog survived but needed thirty stitches. There was also springer spaniel who found £30 million of drugs and another dog that had been trained to add and subtract.

🍂 STRAIGHT RIVERS AND WOBBLY LINES 🍂

Some things in life are better with curves and others are better off being straight. A curved arrow for example would be of little use, whereas a straight boomerang would somewhat defy the point. Yet in the New Forest they seem to have got the two concepts confused. The Lymington River is too straight and the road lines in East Boldre were too wobbly.

Lymington River, running from Brockenhurst, through Lymington then out into the English Channel was straightened by the Victorians around 150 years ago to solve a drainage problem – but this is not how it is supposed to be. Rivers meander and wander, their course changes over the centuries as erosion alters the curves that the river takes – so the overly straight Lymington river is far from natural, and this is something that the New Forest National Park Authority has been trying to rectify – they want a natural and healthy habitat. To this end around £300,000 was spent on returning the river to its natural curves – they did this using old maps, aerial photographs and local knowledge. It was part of a much larger six year project looking at works on rivers and mires.

Whilst the river was too straight some newly painted white lines on roads were not straight enough. In East Boldre some new lines were painted, and the white line, at one point, swerved half a metre into the road. At first it was claimed that the deviation was correct, with some locals being happy that something had been done to enforce the 30mph speed limit which was generally ignored – but then two days later the council admitted that the line was in fact meant to be straight, a crease in the map from where it had been folded meant that the number 4.8 had been read as 4.3 … oops!

🍂 UNUSUAL CRITTERS 🍂

With so many different creatures inhabiting the New Forest there are bound to be a few specimens that fall into the category of the unusual and abnormal.

A funny looking pony …

As you wander around you will see a lot of New Forest ponies, and some Shetland ones, maybe even a few others. You will also notice that there is quite a lot of mud around, especially after it has been raining. One pony, a cross between a Shetland pony and a New Forest pony had very short legs and appeared to be much lower down than its neighbours, so much so that people thought it had sunk and was stuck in the mud. In fact, it looked so stuck that multiple people, on separate occasions called the emergency services to inform them of the trouble.

Double duck

As the mantra in George Orwell's Animal Farm goes, 'Four legs good, two legs bad,' and it was, after complaints from the birds, that it was decided that wings too counted as legs. But for one duck, born in February 2007, this would not have been a problem. Stumpy, born on Warawee Duck Farm, had an extremely rare genetic mutation that resulted in him having four legs, instead of the usual two. The extra legs were situated behind the main pair, and remained unused. So unusual was the mutation that Stumpy quickly rose to fame, appearing on television all across the world, and a blog was even started up for him. The last recorded case before Stumpy was in 2002 but the duckling quickly died, never maturing to adulthood; because of this Stumpy was not expected to live very long – yet he did survive and lived on to become a fully grown duck.

Stumpy's owners, fearing that he would not survive in the wild, built him a large pen to run around in, with a female duck named Alice for company. But whilst roaming he caught one of his legs which became badly broken and had to be removed – leaving nothing but a stump behind, somewhat apt considering his name.

There was so much interest about the duck's mutation that the University of Chicago requested a DNA sample for study, and when the duck was tested for Avian flu a spare sample was sent out to them – who knows what cures may arise from the four-legged duck.

❧ WATCH YOUR STEP … ❧

The New Forest is a wonderful place to walk, but sometimes you need to be careful where you tread …

Cattle grids

These are dotted around towns in the National Park and have a vital role in the day-to-day running of the forest. Their job is to keep animals confined to a certain area whilst still allowing cars to cross, and usually there are gates by the sides for pedestrians – you will not be expected to walk across a cattle grid unless you want to. But in October of 2009 a woman, in Mill Lane in Brockenhurst, got her foot caught in one such cattle grid. The sixty-five-year-old had to be rescued by twenty fireman who took thirty minutes to get her free.

In 2007 firefighters also had to be called out to a cattle grid, again near Brockenhurst, where a horse had become stuck whilst trying to cross one. The animal had to be sedated by a vet before it was cut free – this horse was lucky, so often when trapped the poor animals can panic and break limbs, often having to be put down. This horse though was fine, being brought round after it had been freed.

One wrong foot

There are many large areas of mud and boggy land over the forest, where one can sink extremely quickly if not careful.

In 2006 a man was stranded near Beaulieu Road Station when out for a walk in the New Forest after he became stuck in a bog. The fire services had to be called – yet they found themselves unable to free him. Left with little other choice, they called the Solent coastguard, who airlifted him to safety – the helicopter dragged him up and out of the mud.

In 2005 a group of two women and two children got stuck in the mud up to their thighs in Busket Wood near Lyndhurst – thankfully they had their mobile phones on them and were able to call for assistance – it took firemen twenty minutes to pull each of them out. If they had not had their phones they would have been at risk of hypothermia and therefore potentially of dying.

Not exactly a rabbit hole

Everyone knows that there can be a world of adventure down animal holes, but one dog named Lucy was not lucky enough to find a magical world; instead, he got trapped when he decided to explore a badger sett in Burley in the New Forest, going 2.4m down into the badgers' abode. His owners, worried that he had not returned, contacted the local fire department who came out with listening equipment and a snake-eye camera – but there was no sign of the dog. Yet four days later his owners heard a whimper coming from the badgers' home and the firemen were called back to the scene. This time they turned up with a special license to partly dig up the sett, removing just enough of the earth around the opening for the dog to make his way out to safety – and apart form a bald patch from burrowing he was perfectly healthy, even wagging his tail upon seeing his owners.

Going for a swim

It is not unusual for animals to go swimming, but a 350kg Aberdeen Angus had a little trouble when it went for a paddle in the river Beaulieu, just off Buckler's Hard. The ox ran out of steam and found himself stuck in some mud. After four days the emergency services were called in to intervene.

On closer investigation it was revealed that the animal was not physically trapped or stuck, it was simply exhausted and unable to continue. The fire service, with the help of the Harbour Master, attached a leash around its neck and it was swum back to shore. It was grateful to be returned to its herd.

🌺 A BIT OF SPEED 🌺

Of course, it is not just pigs that are raced in the New Forest. You already know about the annual Pony race that occurs, usually on Boxing Day, but there are other races and feats of speed that take place in the Forest, some of them even making pig racing look like a normal event.

How fast do you mow your grass?

There have been competitions to show mowing prowess, how quickly and neatly you can mow your lawn, and there are regular ploughing contests. But it is only recently that people have been more concerned with not how quickly you can cut grass, but how quickly your lawnmower can go.

In 2008 an American by the name of Bob Cleveland set the first ever lawnmower world land speed record, reaching a slightly crazy speed of 80mph. But this was not deemed fast enough by some, if you can make a lawnmower travel at 80mph then why would anybody want to stop there?

So it was that at the Beaulieu Motor Museum project Runningblade was announced. Done by the team who recently broke the Steam-powered World Land Speed Record (who reached a speed of 139 miles per hour – breaking the longest-standing land speed record), they are hoping to reach triple figures, breaking the 100 miles per hour barrier with a lawnmower.

The lawnmower will be driven by Don Wales, the nephew of the famous Donald Campbell, who holds multiple records. The target speed of 100mph will be hard to reach, it means taking the lawnmower, which must still be able to mow the grass, across one mile in just 36 seconds. The biggest challenge is the risk of the vehicle flipping, as it cannot be the same shape and design as a normal car. It is no small undertaking, and required the work of serious scientist and industry specialists – from aerodynamics experts to fuel specialists.

The project raised funds for Great Ormond Street Hospital and Wessex Heartbeat and the attempt was made on 22-23 May 2010. Wales reached 87.8mph, failing to break the 100mph barrier, but substantially beating the previous record.

Pedal Power

Slightly closer to normality is the pedal-car race that is held in Ringwood Town Centre that can attract 3,000-10,000 spectators. The British Pedal Car Grand Prix is a two-hour race that is held every two years in July. Each lap is 1.4km and some teams spend up to a year building their cars.

❧ UNSCRUPULOUS SCOUNDRELS ❧
AND WRONGFUL ARRESTS

Everywhere in the country plays host to crime of some description and the New Forest has been the scene of some interesting happenings.

Bee Rustling

It is not unknown for cows to go missing, cattle can fetch a good price, and it is a crime that has gone back a long time. But the spate of thefts of bee hives is rather more unusual. Bee hives in the New Forest have been going missing as the price of honey, and therefore the bees, has been going up in recent years. Bee populations over the country have been declining for various reasons which, through basic supply and demand, has upped their value. But, unlike with cattle theft, you need to know what you are doing if you are going to take a beehive. Specialist equipment and knowledge is needed meaning it cannot just be opportunist thieves looking to make a quick buck.

A British bumble bee feeding on the nectar from a lavender plant.

Not a merry Christmas

It is a well known fact that Father Christmas lives in Lapland and in 2008 Lapland happened to be in the New Forest.

The resort, opened by two brothers, was a short-lived affair that was located in Matchams in the New Forest. It was advertised as a winter wonderland, with ice skating, realistic fake snow, real log cabins and huskies. Long before it opened tickets were available on their website at a cost of £30 for a single ticket, or £25 if you were going as part of a group.

However, within days of it opening hundred of complaints had been made. Upon entering, visitors were disappointed with what they saw, saying that the log cabins were simply green sheds, that the tunnel of light was some fairy lights that had been put up in some trees and that the huskies were chained up in a pen. The nativity scene was painted onto a wall. Some people described the park as a joke, whilst others likened it to hell. The ice-skating rink did not work and people were generally unhappy. So much so that six days after it opened the park closed due to the complaints and so much media attention – a lot of people were left with tickets that had been paid for but no park to visit, and many of those that had been were searching for a refund. All in all £1.2 million's worth of tickets were sold to the public. One woman alone spent over £3,000.

The owners claimed that the whole thing was orchestrated by 'professional trouble makers' and their having to close was down to sabotage and a few organised people who wanted them to fail. Yet all in all some 5,000 registered complaints and sought advice. Three Facebook groups were created about the dislike for the park. One of the security guards resigned in shame after just a few days – the turning point for him was when he saw a family who had taken their mother for a day out from the hospice. She was suffering from terminal cancer and was to spend what was likely her last Christmas at Lapland.

The park closed down, the company went into liquidation and nine charges of misleading customers were brought against the brothers. All in all it was not a happy Christmas for the New Forest.

Postal Theft

The postal service in the UK has been struggling for a while, with cut backs and closures of smaller post offices around the country. One such post office in Sway was not helped by a New Forest sub-postmaster who, between November 2003 and July 2006, stole over £55,000. On two occasions he phoned the police, claiming that the post office had been burgled while he had been on the loo. He denied all charges but was found guilty in July of 2007.

Stolen Birds

It seems that in the New Forest it is both the birds and the bees that are at risk – with some people who were supposed to be looking after rare birds taking advantage of their position.

The New Forest Owl Sanctuary in Ringwood was investigated by the police, although the investigation was eventually put on hold. But eighteen months later, in 2003, the BBC's *Inside Out* sent an undercover reporter into the sanctuary to see how the birds were being treated. The reporter, who went in as a volunteer, filmed the conditions that the birds lived in and what happened to ones that were sick. The show claimed that 'knocking' had been occurring, that is to say that sick birds were killed by having their heads banged against a solid surface such as a wall or concrete floor, instead of being put down by a vet supplied lethal injection.

Following this information the police, with the help of the RSPCA raided the sanctuary along with two other buildings including a private residence. One man was arrested, Bruce Berry, the owner. He denied all accusations but the following year he was found guilty of stealing a saker falcon (an extremely rare bird),

A kestrel surveying its kingdom.

selling two marsh harriers and a tawny owl without a license to do so and also displaying birds without a license. He was sentenced to 240 hours of community service and fined £10,000.

The park closed in July 2003 and changed ownership. It underwent a drastic overhaul and is now open as Liberty's Owl, Raptor and Reptile Centre.

Noisy rooster

Not all offences in the New Forest are of such an extreme nature. One such occurrence were the complaints about one Rocky the rooster, who was so loud he was disturbing the peace with his noisy morning calls. The owner, in an attempt to avoid a £5,000 fine tried blacking out the windows of the cockerel's house to try and hide the sunrise from him.

Playful children

Not only were roosters deemed too noisy but in a 100–year–old Scout hut in Ringwood in the New Forest the noise of twelve children playing was too much to bear and they were the cause of a petition signed by thirty-eight residents. The centre was used as a setting for children to meet up who were not in state education. Being home-schooled meant that they were missing out on normal social interaction that is so important to the proper development of children. The vicar of the Avon River Church therefore set up the group, but complaints ensued. The local council asked for them to apply for planning permission for the change of use, which they then denied. Sadly the children had to go home.

Missing mushrooms

Under the English code of mushroom picking, people are allowed to pick up to 1.5kg of mushrooms for personal use – and the New Forest is a great place for mushroom picking. But what happens when you pick more? Or try and sell them? In 2002 a fifty-nine-year-old woman found out. The woman, who had been picking mushrooms for thirty years, was arrested in November 2002 and a kingly sum of £27 of brown Chanterelles was confiscated from her. The Forestry Commission, responsible for the management of the forest land, decided to bring criminal charges against her.

However, Judge John Boggis threw out the case, saying there would be no trial and that the very notion of there being criminal charges in what should be nothing more than a civil case was ludicrous, not to mention a waste of tax payers' money. The Forestry Commission was ordered to pay costs, which were believed to be

Probably not worth getting arrested over.

in the six-figure range. In 2006 she was granted a personal license to pick as many mushrooms as she wanted and to sell them on, this was due to customary law, which, seeing as she had been doing it for over twenty years, meant that she could continue to do so.

Mystery men

In an echo of Brusher Mills, the famous Brockenhurst snake catcher, a mysterious man who had shunned the normal social conventions died at the age of seventy-three in Lymington in June 2007. He had spent the last two years of his life living in New Forest woodland under a tarpaulin sheet. Very little is known about him, with police unable to account for over fifty years of his life. It is known that he went to Red Hill School for Maladjusted Boys in Kent, where lessons were optional, that he did National Service in 1952 and he spent most of his life living rough. Even at the school he had lived in a decrepit old caravan that had once belonged to gypsies – he lived there with a friend and his friend's goat. Even when the door came off during a particularly cold winter he did not move on; doors and beds were an indulgence that he did not really need.

Despite his choice of lifestyle, Albert Van Best, known locally as Yan, was well liked by people. He was described as gentle, educated man with a love of the outdoors. He died of a heart attack, and the coroner ruled natural causes.

❧ NOW THAT'S JUST STRANGE ... ❧

Frogger

Every year brave volunteers in Ringwood risk the roads at night to help the easily squashed toads cross the roads. Wearing high visibility jackets and carrying buckets they search for toads at the roadside and then help them to cross the potentially dangerous traffic and save them from being run over.

They work from February to April every year, helping toads cross and putting up road signs warning users of their and the toads' presence.

The scheme, run by Ringwood Amphibian Conservationists is called 'Toads on Roads'. They saved over 12,000 toads in 2008 and have operated for twenty years. They have the support of the local Planning, Town & Environment Committee.

They are always looking for new volunteers and can be contacted on 01425 478891.

In 2009 the British Tree Climbing Championships was held in the New Forest.

Tree climbing

The 2009 British Tree Climbing Championship was held on the Foxlease estate near Lyndhurst, with a 24.7m tree climbed for the final. Many of the competitors are tree surgeons and the winner, who was also World Tree Climbing Champion, was Jo Hedger, a New Forest resident from Sway.

Making Money

In the first decade of the new millennium there were a spate of floods across the UK. In 2003 one farmer in the New Forest decided to turn this to his advantage. After using his tractor to rescue a stuck motorist from the road adjacent to his land, the grateful driver gave him a thank you in the form of a monetary reward. This gave him an idea. Putting up a sign with his mobile number on, he offered his services as a rescueman. At £35 per rescue he made £455 in three days rescuing thirteen vehicles from the flood water. He even told the tax man of his new earnings.

Not in our town

Lymington is a picturesque town in the New Forest and it is well known for its beautiful Georgian High Street. When the economic crisis hit its Woolworths store closed and was replaced with a 99p store. This in itself was not the problem, but what a local town councillor did not like was the sign that adorned the shop front. He was the first, but not the last, to complain.

Due to the fact that they did not have the proper planning permission for its size or illumination the new owners had to take the sign down and change it, a pleasing technicality for those who had voiced their complaints. However, to appease those that were unhappy with the original sign a competition for a new design was held, with a student at Brockenhurst College winning. The new sign, using his design is now visible above the shop and it appears that everyone is happy.

Not enough trees

Ever year Christmas swings around. There are many things that one does, and many traditions that people feel the need to fulfil. One such tradition is the Christmas tree. The Forestry Commission sells Christmas trees at sites in Brockenhurst and Moors Valley Country Park, all the trees are grown sustainably within the Forest, yet the New Forest found itself in the rather strange position of having run out of trees. Their 3,000 trees were quickly sold, leaving many customers disappointed. Part of the rush on New Forest trees was the shift in attitudes, more people wanted accountability, knowing where there trees had come from and that they had been produced ethically – something the New Forest trees were well known for.

A happier Christmas

One Bournemouth resident decided to buy a whopping 50ft tree from the New Forest. And, in what must have been a very strange sight, he towed the tree home on a trailer attached to a tiny G-Wiz.

The 50ft tree had to be cut into sections to be fit into different rooms in the house. It took three days and ten people to put it up, with a crane being used to put the final piece on the roof of his house.

four

THE BIRDS
AND THE BEES

A kestrel circled high over head, looking for something to eat, gliding on the warm air, sharp eyes scanning the ground. A man was standing dejected, next to something, but this was of no interest to him – a man was too big to eat, and too often, for reasons unknown to him, they would try to hurt him.

The man looked up, a kestrel was high up in the air above him, looking for food no doubt. Normally he would take a moment to watch the bird in flight, a majestic creature … but today was different. He turned his attention back to the beehive in front of him. It did not bode well, not for him or his family.

He double checked – these sort of things were worth checking, you had to be sure. He lifted off the top once more, hoping beyond hope he would hear the sound of hundreds of bees going about their business … but no; it was empty. The bees had gone. This only meant one thing. Bees were like rats, and just as rats would leave a sinking ship bees would leave a dying man. He probably would not have long now. He looked down to his feet – it was a blessing really. Unlike most people he had been given advanced warning. He could sort out his affairs, and, more importantly, he could say goodbye to his family.

So far you have learnt about deer and boars, falcons and hares. There are, however, a myriad of other bird, insect and animal species that exist in the New Forest, some are every day occurrences, whilst others are rare and obscure. Below are a selection of these different creatures and how they play a part in the complex life of the National Park.

🌿 BADGERS 🌿

Today they are more commonly seen, at least by most people, as road kill rather than in their natural habitat. Even though most people have never seen one, as they are not as common in suburbia as they once were, they are easily identified due to their unique shape and colouring. The word badger possibly comes from the French word *bêchur* meaning digger, which would have been introduced to the English language by William the Conqueror.

Living in setts, they occupy networks of underground tunnels and small chambers and will often live in a multi-generational unit. Even though they look bulky their main source of food is earthworms, eating several hundred in a day, though they will pretty much eat anything small, from frogs to acorns.

During the Middle Ages badger baiting was a popular past time. The badger would have been attacked by dogs, with people betting on the outcomes, something that is, of course, illegal today. The dachshund (meaning Badger Dog) was originally bred to be sent down into a sett to locate the badger so that it could be extracted – this was known as badger digging. The latter was only outlawed in 1973. Today the badger has special protection, beyond the Wildlife and Country Side Act, in the form of the Protection of Badgers Act of 1992. It is an offence to kill a badger or interfere with a sett without a license from Natural England.

The best time to see a badger is at dawn or dusk when they leave their setts in search of food.

❀ SQUIRRELS ❀

Just as in the rest of the country, grey squirrels are very common in the New Forest and are considered a pest by many. The Wildlife and Countryside Act 1981, which has usually been cited in this book as protecting animals, makes it illegal to release a grey squirrel if it is trapped. It must be killed in a humane manner.

They live in dreys in trees, made of small twigs and branches, and quite unexpectedly their young are refereed to as kittens. You will have no trouble seeing them around the New Forest, though the ones in towns and cities tend to be easier to spot and far more approachable.

They are best known for causing the decline of the native Red Squirrel, currently it is estimated there are 2.5 million grey squirrels in Britain compared to around 140,000 Red Squirrels – if you want to see Red Squirrels in the area the nearest places are the Isle of Wight (visible from the New Forest) and on Brownsea Island (a small island in Poole Harbour).

❧ FOXES ❧

Another animal that is common both in and outside of the New Forest is the fox – normally seen skulking along the road in the early hours of the morning, the New Forest offers them a more natural habitat. For many years they were hunted and they are still very much seen as a pest due to their interference with livestock.

❧ BIRDS ❧

The diversity of the New Forest habitats lead to a rich and varied bird life – the combination of open heathland, woodland, wetland and rivers give home to the majority of Britain's bird species.

Among birds of prey you have the sparrowhawk, buzzard, hobbies, kestrels and the more rare honey buzzard. Kestrels are easy to spot as they can often be seen hovering just before diving down to capture their prey.

These birds are protected by law, to such an extent that any trees to be felled must be checked for nests – if they are found then the trees cannot be touched until the young have left. The Forestry Commission, in partnership with the RSPB, have installed cameras in different bird of prey nests – this footage is on show in the New

A stonechat making its distinctive call – so named as it sounds like two stones being hit together.

A bird that is hard to miss in the forest, a male chaffinch.

Forest Museum. A live camera of a goshawk nest can also be seen at the New Forest Reptile Centre two miles south of Lyndhurst. It is a free attraction and you can also see all of the UK's reptiles while you are there.

On a trip around the Forest you can also spot hen harriers and tawny owls. There is also a large variety of wetland and other birds such as the snipe, curlew, redshank and lapwing – the latter have one of the most distinctive calls in the bird family, a 'pee-wit' noise that can be heard from a great distance. The male lapwing can often be heard shrieking whilst diving around erratically near its nest on the forest floor.

A few birds in the New Forest nest on the ground, in open heathland. These are suffering more and more from recreational users and their dogs – it is important that during the nesting season (March and April) dogs are kept under control, especially around open heath. During this time they must be kept to the paths.

Another unmistakable bird, from its song, is the stonechat, so named as it sounds like two stones being hit together. Other woodland birds that you can expect to see include bullfinches, tits, magpies, wood pigeons (bigger than their town counterparts, with a lower beating noise of their wings – they can often be heard almost crashing out of trees as they are not the most delicate of animals when taking off). And there is of course the ever-present crow. Along the larger rivers you will also find swans, both the standard white ones and the odd black one on the Beaulieu Estate.

About three quarters of all Dartford Warblers, a small rare bird, exist in the New Forest. The bird get its name from Dartford Heath in Kent from which the bird died out in the early twentieth century, and it was thought at one point they would become extinct within Britain – but they have found somewhat of a stronghold in the New Forest. A good place to view them is in the woodland and heath around Beaulieu Road railway station – though they are small and quick, making them hard to spot!

🐛 INSECTS AND INVERTEBRATES 🐛

Yet again, the numerous habitats in the New Forest means that it is swarming with different species of insect – according to the Forestry Commission of all British invertebrates 46 per cent of beetles, 74 per cent of dragonflies and damselflies and 67 per cent of crickets and grasshoppers can be found in the New Forest, that gives a total of around 10,000 different within the National Park. Most of them can be found in the dead wood that is so common in the area.

Some notable examples are the stag beetle and the New Forest Cicada. The stag beetle is distinct due to its stag like antlers, which they use for fighting. At 5cm long they are the largest beetle in Britain – some non-native species of stag beetle can reach up to 12cm in length! They play an important role in the life of the forest, with their larvae eating dead wood for over a year before emerging in beetle form. In the summer they can be seen flying around and are easily recognisable due to their size. They are good subjects for photographs as, upon seeing a large object moving, they tend to stay perfectly still, giving you time to take a photo – of course try not to take too long and to bother it too much. In medieval times the beetles would have been caught and flown on a length of thread … something that would probably have been a rather interesting sight!

The New Forest Cicada is the only member of the cicada family that is native to Britain and it can only be found amongst the trees of the New Forest. The song of the New Forest Cicada, normally the most distinctive feature of the cicada family, is of such a high pitch that most people cannot hear it.

The relatively warm summers and proximity to Europe also means you get a variety of non-native insects occasionally finding their way over, such as the hummingbird hawk moth.

Ladybirds are neither rare nor exciting, but most of us have a soft spot for these creatures; they are, for an insect, incredibly cute. Their proper name is the slightly less endearing Coccinedlliade. There are roughly 5,000 species worldwide. The most common one is

If you look carefully in the grass you can see a wide variety of different insects roaming around.

A British seven spotted ladybird.

Best not to get stung.

the seven-spotted ladybird, easy enough to identify from its seven spots. Legend has it that during the Middle Ages crops were being destroyed and the farmers, with no way of controlling the pests that were causing so much damage, prayed to the Virgin Mary. Suddenly thousands of the now named ladybirds descended on the fields, saving the crops. Today they are still valued for the pest-control abilities.

Bees also play an important roll not only for the New Forest, but for the whole global ecosystem. Bees are responsible for pollination and the bumblebee is instantly recognisable to everyone. The other role played by bees is the production of honey.

What most people do not realise is that there are over 20,000 species of bee world wide, seven of which are honey bees – the bumble bee not being one of them.

Honey production is quite fruitful in the New Forest; the generally milder winters allow a longer bee-keeping season and the range of different flowers and heathers means that honey production fairs slightly better in the area.

Bee stings can be surprisingly painful, but bees only sting in defence. Unless you have an allergic reaction to the sting all you need to do is simply remove the sting as soon as possible (the longer it is in the more poison is introduced into your body). If, however, you do have an allergic reaction then you should call an ambulance immediately (still taking out the sting), similarly if you are stung in the mouth or near an eye you should seek medical attention. The largest number of stings in one go ever recorded was 2,243. The unfortunate person made a full recovery!

Local folklore has it that your bees will know when you are about to die and will leave the hive – an empty hive was something that no one would want to come home to. Though today the bee population is in serious decline, both in the UK and worldwide, something that could likely lead to problems as there are fewer and fewer insects around to pollinate plants.

🌸 REPTILES AND AMPHIBIANS 🌸

One of the snakes that can be found in Britain, one of only three species, is the adder (*Vipera berus*). It is the only poisonous snake in Britain. Even though its bite is venomous it is not considered a dangerous species due to weak nature of the venom and the way it behaves; since 1876 there have only been fourteen recorded fatalities, the last of which was a five-year-old child in 1975. Even though it is unlikely to kill a healthy adult, you can guarantee that it will hurt and can still make you feel very unwell for a few days and on top of this some people can have an adverse and serious reaction. It is therefore important to seek medical advice straight away. People being bitten is not a very common occurrence, this is because they will only strike when startled and alarmed; if you come across one simply leave it alone, it will most likely do the same to you, they are not naturally aggressive, or even brave, creatures.

The adder is 60 to 90cm long and weighs up to 1.8kg. It hibernates for up to half the year and breeds every three years. They are what is known as ovoviviparious – this means that the young grow in eggs but inside the body, being born live, three to twenty at a time. Adders usually give birth in the late summer. They feed on small mammals such as mice, as well as birds, lizards and amphibians. Due to their need for basking, foraging and hibernation they require a varied habitat, such as that offered by the New Forest. Under the

The adder, Britain's only poisonous snake.

The smooth snake can be incredibly hard to spot.

The common lizard basking in the sun.

1981 Wildlife and Countryside Act is illegal to kill, harm, injure or sell adders.

The grass snake (*Natrix natrix*) likes to be near water, feeding on amphibians, usually the common frog and toad. The toads are fairly large compared to the diameter of the snakes, so the snakes tend to be fairly stationary after eating, unable to move efficiently or quickly – they eat their prey live and whole, with no use of constriction or poison.

Grass snakes are the UK's largest reptile, and can grow to 2m in length, though they are usually more around the 1m mark. But despite their far greater length, they weigh less than adders due to a much lower girth – they weigh in at about 240g. They are usually dark green or brown in colour, with a yellow ring just below the head. They lay eggs in June or July, which take ten weeks to hatch, requiring a temperature of at lest 21°C, this is why they often use decaying, composting heaps of material, which provide the necessary temperature and humidity.

They are preyed on by owls and foxes, relying on two defence mechanisms to survive. The first is the age-old trick of playing dead. The other is to secrete a garlic smelling fluid – they rarely bite.

The final species of snake that is found in the New Forest is the smooth snake (*Coronella austriaca*), which is the smallest of the three snakes coming in at 55-75cm. They are brown and grey, with bits of reddish brown, they can be told apart from the adder due to their thinner body. Like the grass snake, they are harmless to people. They feed on sand lizards, slow worms and insects, sometimes by coil constriction. They hibernate between October and April.

The most famous story to do with snakes is undoubtedly the life of one Brusher Mill, a snake catcher in the new forest, he is so famous in fact that he has his own section in this book (*see* 'The snake catcher').

All of Britain's native reptiles can also be found in the New Forest including the common frog and toad and three species of newt. The successfully reintroduced sand lizard can also be seen – it can be spotted in a few places on the west of the Forest.

The New Forest's range of habitats has led to it being an important safe haven for reptiles and amphibians – all of the species found in the Forest can be viewed at the New Forest Reptile Centre (*see* 'Places to Visit').

✿ TALES OF TREES AND OTHER PLANTS ✿

> *The forest had not seen weather like this in years, even the old trees had trouble recalling something worse. Only the Old Yew, the oldest tree in the whole of the forest spoke of something from the old days, before the Normans, before the other trees were born. The winds gusted through their leaves, bending their branches back. The older trees stood tall and firm, bending but not breaking, they would weather this, they weathered everything. The youngsters tried to be brave, but the winds worried them, their roots did not run as deep or as far as their elders ... the wind worried them.*
>
> *The weather changed, the stormed picked up, a new anger, a new vigour entered into it. The winds no longer gushed through the forest, they tore. Branches no longer bent, they broke, trees no longer swayed, they fell. Everywhere trees were being uprooted. It was as if the weather wanted to destroy the forest, and it was doing a good job.*

A forest would not be much of a forest without trees – certainly the Forestry Commission would be somewhat out of a job. In the Forest at War section you have already seen how the trees of the New Forest played a fundamental part in defending our nation and that they are at the backbone of what makes the New Forest what it is. The National Park contains countless different species of trees and plants and in this section we will look at some of the more interesting ones and the tales they could tell.

The Knightwood Oak

This is the largest oak in the New Forest, sometimes known by its other name, the Queen of the Forest. It has a girth of 7.4m at its base and, at 2.4m across, it is wide enough to drive a car through.

Some consider it to be the oldest tree at just over 500 years old. Due to the amount of visitors it receives, the tree is now surrounded by a fence to stop too much soil compaction happening around its roots. In February 2006 the Forestry Commission harvested some cuttings from the tree to create some offspring with identical genes. The tree is also a good example of pollarding, the traditional way of collecting wood without killing the tree. This is the process where you cut the trunk to within a meter or two off the ground, encouraging the tree to grow out in several large branches, increasing the amount of wood that can be harvested. This practice was stopped

*The most well-known
tree in the Forest*

when the Royal Navy started using oaks for ship building – one long, solid trunk was better suited for cutting into planks.

Several other oaks have been planted and named nearby the Knightwood Oak. They are the Millennium Oak, planted by the chief ranger Joyce Sortwell in 2000; the Queen's Oak, planted by Her Majesty the Queen on 12 April 1979 to celebrate the nine hundred year anniversary of the Forest; and the Deputy Surveyor's Oak, a sapling from the Knightwood Oak, planted in memory of Don Small who was Forestry Commission Deputy Surveyor from 1971–1983.

It is easy to visit, with a car park a couple of minutes away from it. It is a nice place for a picnic and you will pass it if you are going to the Bolderwood deer sanctuary – it is not far from Lyndhurst.

The Eagle Oak

Not too far the Knightwood Oak, hidden away in its inclosure is the Eagle Oak. It is so named when in 1810 a New Forest keeper shot and killed a Sea Eagle from its branches. But this was not just any kill; this was the last Sea Eagle in the Forest and within 100 years there were no more Sea Eagles in Britain. However, from the 1970s the species has been reintroduced to the small Islands around Scotland, though the growth of their population has been somewhat hampered by theft of their eggs. Hopefully though, with time, this member of the eagle family, a close relative of the bald eagle, will one day again fly between the trees of the New Forest.

The oldest tree

There is some dispute over this. Some claim that it is the Knightwood Oak (the proponents of this claiming that the large oak tree is an impressive 1,000 years old, although it is more likely to be around the 500-year-old mark). Most, however, would agree that the title of the New Forest's Oldest Tree would go to a common yew found in Brockenhurst church, which may be up to 1,000 years old. Whoever the victor may have been they would have survived the Great Storm of 1703, in which it is estimated that around 4,000 oaks were knocked down. At the same time the Royal Navy lost thirteen ships, and around 8,000-15,000 people were killed. It was the worst ever storm to hit southern England.

The tallest tree

The tallest tree in the Forest is a Wellingtonia (better known as a giant sequoia) in the Rhinefield Ornamental Drive. Planted in 1852 it has now reached the lofty height of 55m. If you fancy talking a look then you can always take the New Forests Tall Tree Walk. While far from the tallest tree, the largest beechwood in the Forest is the Mark Ash Wood.

The use of trees

In the Forest at War section you saw how the trees played an important part in defending our nation in the form of supplying the wood to the Royal Navy for shipbuilding. The felling of trees did not stop with the navy though and the New Forest is still used

Some trees are felled for safety reasons, as was this one which was by the side of a road.

for timber production today – though of course the methods have changed somewhat over the centuries, instead of axes there are chainsaws, and the equipment, all round, is more advanced and far safer – around 1,000 tonnes can be cut down each week, with a lot of the wood being supplied to local mills, with conifers largely going to produce fencing products. In the winter about 1,000 tones of high-quality hardwood is produced.

The timber production forecast for 1 April 2008 to 31 March 2011 gives 73,560 cubic metres of conifers and 10,154 cubic meters of broad-leaves being felled – that is about 50,000 tonnes of timber each year, or 2,000 lorry loads. All the timber comes from areas that are thinned to promote the growth of the remaining trees, from areas being restored to their original habitat and finally from areas due for replanting. All the wood is FSC marked, meaning that it is certified as being sustainable. Inclosures are harvested on five-year cycles.

To give an idea of how many trees need to be planted to keep up this sustainability, in 2004/5 79,000 were planted, covering 29 hectares.

The New Forest has 100 inclosures covering some 8,500 hectares. Inclosures are areas of land fenced off to keep out commoners' animals which can damage young trees. They are important for timber production as well as conservation and recreation.

Now the Forestry Commission has a new mission, instead of creating a strategic wood reserve in event of war they are now aiming to replace the fast-growing conifers with hard wood trees – even though the conifers are a good source of income for the

Forest they are mostly species that are not native to the UK, and so are being replaced.

🌺 MORE THAN JUST TREES 🌺

Of course, it goes without saying that there is a lot more to the forest than just trees. Even if you narrow the field to plants then there are still countless other things to see in the New Forest. Here are just a few examples of what you can see on your jaunts around the New Forest. Remember that no matter how pretty some of the flowers seem you should not pick them – some are rare and endangered; leave them where they are for everyone to enjoy.

The Woodland

Blue Bells – Often found covering inclosure floors like a soft blue blanket, they are most abundant in May. The cycle path between New Park in Brockenhurst and Bank is a fantastic place to get a good view of these colourful flowers.

Bugle – Growing in sunny damp sites, this can be seen over the whole of the Forest.

Foxgloves – A plant that has been used in medicine for hundreds of years. Until recently it was the source for the drug digitalis, coming from the foxgloves' Latin name *Digitalis purpurea*. At 1.5m tall with purple flowers akin to the bluebell, they are not easy to miss and are mostly found at the edge of woodland or in areas that have recently been felled.

Common dog violet – Growing in sunny areas, they are important for the rare species of butterfly, the pearl-bordered fritillary.

Heathland

As already mentioned, heathland is in need of conservation, with the New Forest being one of the key areas where it occurs. Below are a few of the plants that can be found.

Gorse – This plant is common around the forest and is actually found in three species. The most noticeable and well known is, unsurprisingly, common gorse. Its large spikes are designed to offer protection but they do not deter the ponies who happily munch

Oddly enough, gorse flowers smell of coconuts.

Heather is an extremely important habitat and the New Forest has one of the largest collections in Europe.

As pretty as flowers may seem, they should not be picked. It is better to leave them in place for everyone to see – you never know how rare they might be!

away at it, even though it looks rather painful to eat! At points in the past it was actually cut and used to feed ponies. The yellow flowers, oddly enough, smell of coconut. The other two species of gorse are western gorse and dwarf gorse.

Heather – This is the plant most associated with heathland. The four species found in the forest are an important source of nectar for bees, a fact often exploited by honey producers. The four species found are true heather (also known as ling), bell heather, the cross-leaved heath, and Dorset heath, the rarest. Though the latter is not easy to spot, it can be seen in a few very wet areas.

Orchids – Another unmistakable plant that can be found at the edge of heathland in the case of the common spotted orchid and the heath spotted orchid, whilst the southern marsh orchid, as the name suggests, occurs in areas where the heathland turns into marshland.

Wild Gladiolus – This is, in some ways, the New Forest's crowning glory, it is the only place in Britain where it grows wild. They tend to grow on the edge of pasture woodlands. It is rare and only flowers for a short time in the summer, making it quite hard to spot.

Coral Necklace – This plant gets its name from the flowers, which look like a necklace made of coral. They grow close to the ground in damp patches.

Wetland

The third type of habitat in the Forest is wetland, and is again home to many different types of flora.

Bog cotton – This is what common cotton grass is known as locally and is found growing in, as you can probably guess, bogs. There is also a second species of cotton grass, slender cotton grass, which is much rarer.

Marsh Gentian – Growing in wetland areas, it blooms in the summer and is common around the New Forest. Its flowers are bright blue.

Sundew – They live in wet soil that, like most of the soil in the New Forest, is poor in nutrients. They are carnivorous plants that supplement their diet by digesting small insects that land on the sticky hairs that cover their leaves.

One of the many different grasses and reeds that you can see around the Forest.

Bog Asphodel – Another wetland flower than blooms in the summer. The Latin name, *Narthecium ossifragum* means bone breaker, coming from the old belief by farmers that if a cow ate one its legs would break. This is not as ridiculous as it sounds and not that far from the truth. Whilst the plant itself will not contribute to the cow's legs breaking, if it were a large part of its diet it would cause a problem. This is because the plant grows in a low nutrient area and there is little calcium in it, and as such the cow would not get enough in its diet, causing its bones to weaken.

Butterwort – The New Forest is a little backwards in regards to this plant, with the common butterwort being rare and the rarer pale butterwort being more common. Both can be found growing in bogs.

Bog Orchid – Again, as the name suggests, it is found in bogs, though it is extremely rare and, at about 5cm high, it is very hard to spot.

Foreign Invaders and Unwelcome Natives

One of the big drives of the current plans in managing the New Forest, both in terms of woodland and as a National Park is its restoration to as natural a state as possible – this has been seen in the Forestry Commission's desire to replace conifers, over time, with hard wood specimens. Another area that is being dealt with concerns a few other plants that have found their way into the New Forest, but are unwelcome visitors.

Four such plants, Japanese knotweed, Himalayan balsam, giant hogweed and American skunk cabbage started off in people's gardens as ornamental plants and flowers. But, having escaped the confines of domestic life, they have made their way to the Forest where they threaten natural species, which in turn puts local wildlife at risk. Whether it be butterflies and bees missing out on nectar or other rare plants loosing out to the competition, it is something that is trying to be addressed. The Non-Native Plant Project, run by the Hampshire and Isle of Wight Wildlife Trust, the Environmental Agency, the Department for Agricultural and Rural Affairs (DEFRA), the Forestry Commission, Natural England as well as the New Forest National Park Authority was set up in 2004 to control five species. The other one, not on the above list, is the New Zealand Pygmyweed, which was introduced into ponds as an oxygenator.

If you fancy helping out they are always on the look out for volunteers – check them out at http://www.hwt.org.uk/pages/new-forest-non-native-plants-project.html for more information.

Another big problem within the New Forest is the ragwort – a bright yellow flower, akin in looks to the daisy, that causes liver poising in grazing animals. They appear from May to October with each plant producing somewhere in the region of 30,000 to 150,000 seeds – horses will usually not eat the flower, due its bitter taste, but this quickly fades when the flower dries, making it a particular problem for hay products. Sadly, by the time a horse shows noticeable symptoms too much damage has already been done to their liver. Ragwort lives on poor soil, where the seeds can lay dormant for up to fifteen years, and in poor, over-grazed areas where it flourishes and poses a higher risk to livestock, as it is more predominantly a food source.

It is one of the five plants that are controlled by the Weeds Act of 1959 which was passed to stem the spread of the plants. It states that landowners should take measures to stop them spreading, and it allows the Secretary of State for Environment, Food and Rural affairs to make enforcements on private land, including a fine of up to £1,000. The other plants listed are broad-leaved dock, curled dock, creeping thistle and spear thistle.

One natural form of control, that has been used with some success in New Zealand, is the introduction of the Cinnabar moth caterpillars – the larvae eat the leaves and flowers of the ragwort, meaning that it cannot spread and reproduce. While it is not being used in the UK, the Forestry Commission teams that are responsible for the removal of ragwort will leave any of the plants where they find the caterpillars feeding.

Sudden Oak Death

In 2002 *Phytophthoraa ramorum* was first spotted in a garden centre in the UK – it poses a serious threat to forests, where it can lead to the eventual death of trees. The trees that are most at risk in the New Forest are Douglas firs and beech trees. One of the problems is that it can infect rhododendrons, a plant that is populous in the New Forest, particularly on Rhinefield Ornamental Drive. Although it does not kill rhododendrons the plants act as a source from which the disease can spread. As of 2009 it has not yet spread to trees, remaining in bushes, but if it does make the leap it would have serious consequences. Such was the concern that in 2008 dozens of rhododendron bushes were burnt to stop the spread of the deadly spores. Areas of the Forest were also cordoned off to stop animals from spreading the spores but in August of 2009 a new outbreak was detected outside of the cordon.

Fungi

Many people are not really sure what Fungi are, certainly they are not plants. They belong to a separate kingdom all of their own. They are the largest of all known organisms, with the mushrooms and toadstools we see just the fruiting part of a much larger body that connects them underground – the biggest one is thought to be under Yellowstone National Park, covering the whole of the reserve! In the UK you can find around 12,000 different species of fungi, compared with 70,000 worldwide. Of these 12,000 the New Forest is home to some 2,700 different varieties.

Due to the huge number of different types that can be found in the Forest you must make sure you know what you are picking before you do so – this is not to say that you cannot pick something if it is poisonous, but it must not be kept in the same basket as those that are intended for eating. The rules for picking fungi are simple:

- Only collect for personal use, and only up to 1.5kg
- Obey warning signs

Fungi play an important role in the life cycle of the Forest.

- Never remove all of the fungi in one area
- If you do not know what it is, leave it – it might be rare!

Remember, if you are going to eat it, make sure you know exactly what it is, always check the picture carefully against a guidebook, as some can look similar until close inspection. They will also generally go off fairly quickly – if it is something you have not tried before, eat a small bit first – and one more thing, make sure you enjoy!

Some common ones that can be found, both in the New Forest and in the supermarket include oyster mushrooms, penny bun (also known as porcini in Italian) and the chanterelle – there are many other types as well, but these are easy to spot and are great for cooking.

five

ENJOYING
THE FOREST

🌿 EXPLORING THE FOREST 🌿

The forest is a great place, whether you want to go for a walk, a cycle or a ride on a horse – for a short trip or a week's camping it has a lot to offer – but it is always best to go prepared.

It is a good idea to know beforehand what you are after and plan accordingly. Are you going to go to see a particular animal, or do you just fancy a stroll in the country? If you know what it is you want then you are more likely to get the most out of your visit.

How to get there

The best and most environmentally friendly way to get to the New Forest is by train, with stops at many of the places of interest – Brockenhurst, Ashurst New Forest, Beaulieu (though the station, Beaulieu Road, is three and a half miles from the town) and Sway are all within the National Park boundaries. Check www. nationalrail.co.uk or www.thetrainline.co.uk for times and ticket prices. It is worth booking in advance if you can as the fares can be much cheaper, and there are often special promotions. Bicycles are a great way to get around when you are there; you can takes these on the train with you for no extra cost or hire some within the Forest. When cycling in the Forest stick to paths that bikes are allowed on, there are small wooden posts dotted around, telling you where you can and cannot cycle. A helmet is a good idea, the paths can be very uneven and a stray stone might be enough to send you a little off course. If you are going for a long cycle it is worth taking a puncture repair kit with you just in case – make sure you know how to use it!

You can also access the New Forest by road, you can use one of the many online services (such as multimap or google maps) to plan your route. A map is always useful, and if you are strolling off paths then a compass will serve you well. Just like with any long walk, some food and drink would not go amiss. If you do take anything with you make sure you do not leave anything behind, whether it be rubbish or food. A hastily discarded apple core might be enough to give one of the commoner's stock, such as a New Forest Pony, the idea that all visitors might be in the possession of tasty treats –

this in turn might draw them to roads or car parks where they will be more at risk of getting hit.

Another option is the New Forest Tour – this is an hourly bus that does a two-hour tour of the Forest – you can get on and off as many times as you would like in the day, and even take your bike on the bus. It is an open-top bus and includes a guide with money-off vouchers and on-board commentary. It is a good way to cover a lot of the New Forest in a short amount of time, while also taking cars off the road – even if you drive to the New Forest it is a great way to explore once you are there. (*See* 'Places to Visit' for more information about the route and the tour.)

When to go

Just in case you have not guessed yet, when you go depends on what you want to see and what you want to do. If you are after a sighting of a certain animal then consider what time they are out and about. If you want to take pictures then light will be a consideration. It is also a good idea to avoid any busy times of the year if possible. On a busy day, such as Easter Sunday, you will be lucky to spot anything – there are so many people in the Forest, making so much noise, that everything disappears. If you can, the best time will usually be mid week, and a sunny winter's day will always beat a bustling summer one.

The weather and what to wear

An important consideration on any trip is what you wear – it needs to not only be suited to the weather but also to the terrain. Decent shoes are a must – even if it has not been raining you will come across boggy areas and there are streams criss-crossing the forest, so wear something which, at the very least, you do not mind getting caked in mud. Waterproof boots are a good idea; there are few things worse than having to spend the day walking with wet feet. If you are camping waterproof shoes are a must. Wellies are often a good bet and can often be seen worn by locals.

Do not wear anything that you mind getting dirty or scratched, you do not want to ruin an expensive jacket on a stray thorn or on the ever-present gorse. If you are planning on watching deer at dusk be aware that, especially in spring, the temperature can drop quickly at night, and you will also go from walking to standing still – so pack extra layers, you will probably need more than you think. Natural colours are best, something that helps you blend into the forest a little, especially if you want to get any good sightings.

Where to Stay

There are plenty of places to stay in the New Forest, hotels, bed and breakfasts, cottages to hire and camp sites. Camping can be a great way to experience the forest, but you need to stick to designated camp sites – camping in the Forest itself, wild camping, is discouraged (you can do a lot of damage setting up a tent, especially at night, and too many people are tempted to light fires) and you will get moved on by the Forestry Commission. If you are taking a car you will need to book in advance – though if you are on foot you will usually not have a problem just turning up.

Lady luck

There are many factors to consider when trying to catch a glimpse of an animal, time of year and time of day, what the weather is like and what you are wearing, sometimes even what you have eaten (a deer's sense of smell can be uncanny). But even with the most meticulous planning, you will still probably need the help of lady luck.

Lady luck can be a photographer's best friend – you can get that one in a thousand shot that is a perfect ensemble of a hundred small things going right, but as easily as she can smile at you she can also turn and laugh. The first time I tried to photograph red deer at Ober Heath was a disaster for one reason – the Forestry Commission had been out shooting fallow deer that day as part of their measures to control the population. They had shot eleven in total, which, unsurprisingly had scared the red deer, forcing them deeper into the forest and into hiding, leaving none left for me to see.

So just remember, be patient and do not go out with a sighting or a photo being the only aim of the day. To say that my first excursion to Ober Heat was a disaster is more than a little unfair. It was a beautiful spring day, a lovely walk and no matter what you spot you will be greeted by a myriad of animal noises and varying sights that only the New Forest can provide.

Being responsible

When you are exploring, or trying to get that elusive shot, it can be all to easy to unwittingly cause harm. It is important to care about the world around you and enjoy the nature it has to offer whilst leaving it around for others to see in the future, so follow the countryside code, which is summarised briefly as:

- Be safe, plan ahead and follow any signs – think about how long you will be walking for, know roughly where you are going. The New Forest has many criss-crossing paths and unless you have a very good sense of direction it can be easy to get lost. If you are going exploring let someone know where you are going and when you expect to be back, you will almost certainly be fine but you never know. One of the beautiful things about the forest is that you can walk for hours without seeing another person, but in case there is a problem it is best to have a mobile phone on you, reception is generally good across the forest, though best not rely soley on it.

- Leave gates and property as you find them – if a gate is open when you find it leave it that way, if it was closed then close it. It may seem odd for a gate to be left open, but a farmer may have left it that way so that livestock can reach water. If you are walking in a group make sure the last person to go through the gate knows how to leave it. If the gate has instructions on them, make sure they are followed.

- Protect plants and animals and take your litter home; any leftover rubbish can be dangerous to animals and can spread disease. Be careful where you tread, do not pick flowers just because you think they are pretty. If you are going to use a tripod to take a photograph then take particular care if it has spiked legs.

- Keep dogs under close control – dogs can cause damage and scare animals if not controlled properly, and by law you must control your dog to ensure it does not. Near farm animals the dog must be kept on a leash, and on most bits of open country and common land between 1 March and 31 July. On paths you do not have to have them on a lead so long as you can keep them under control. And please, clean up after your dog!

- Consider other people – not really much expansion is needed here. Just be nice!

- The New Forest is always at risk of fire, especially during the summer – avoid the risk of setting a fire at all times. Put out cigarettes properly, do not light fires and only have barbecues in designated areas.

◉ Some other notes – when driving through the New Forest it can be tempting to drive quickly, but be aware that animals can appear suddenly, so keep a look out and drive at appropriate speeds. Slow down for horses, walkers and livestock. Horses have the right of way, even if you are on a bicycle!

❧ A FEW WALKS ❧

The New Forest is a wonderful place to go for a walk, to just lose yourself for a few minutes, hours or even days. This book is not intended as a guidebook for walks, but this section is something to get you started. However, any walk in the Forest will be a nice one, so my advice would be this: just go there, explore and enjoy it.

Brockenhurst

There are two easy walks you can do from Brockenhurst station, and on your way back you can stop for a drink and some food if it takes your fancy.

As you come into the station head up the stairs to take the main exit, then turn right walk along the marked footpath towards the level crossing. Before you reach the main road take the first available left and keep going. You will pass the Thatched Cottage on your right, which serves high-quality food, and then reach a junction with a bank on the corner. Continue straight across and just on the other side you will see the town's old fire bell, standing on the corner just off the road. Continue through the town's high street. This is a great place to see wandering ponies and donkeys blocking traffic, and in the late afternoon and early evening you will often see donkeys standing at gates waiting to be let in by their owners. Keep going past the shops until you hit the ford and take a right. (There is a bridge for pedestrians so you do not have to worry about getting wet!) If you have good eyes and the light is favourable you can often see some small fish swimming in the stream as you walk along and away from the town. Even here it is worth keeping your eyes open for different birds in the trees and bushes around you.

After a few minutes you will come to a patch of open grass in front of you, as the road also continues on – depending on what you want to do you can either take the path cutting through the grass for a nice stroll in the forest, or continue along the road, where, after another half an hour or so, you should get to see some red deer.

If you take the path through the grass it will slowly turn into a gravel path as the grass becomes more wild giving way in places to heather and heathland. If you are lucky you will often see a kestrel hunting to your right, particularly over the thick gorse bushes; there is barren forked trunk that it can often be seen perching on. Over the trees to your right some larger birds of prey can be seen hunting. Ponies and donkeys will also be grazing on the land, whilst numerous smaller birds will be visible, from blue tits to bull finches. If you are lucky, you may catch a glimpse of red or fallow deer who sometimes come out to feed. Rabbits can also be seen, but they tend to be very easily spooked.

The path will eventually lead you to the forest, where you will see a bridge straight in front of you. Taking the bridge, you can either follow the path on to Lyndhurst, or take a right just after the bridge, following a path through the Forest back towards Brockenhurst. It is a great area to wander around and explore, and you are never that far from town.

If you choose to follow the signposts to Lyndhurst you will go through a gate, just past the bridge, and then take a left shortly after this. If you head directly right for a few meters instead you will come to a deer enclosure where you will see fallow deer grazing in the afternoon. It is about three miles to Lyndhurst.

Instead of turning right at the open bit of grass after you have left Brockenhurst you can carry on until you hit open heathland. On this long walk down you will pass the Forest Park Hotel, which played a role in both the First and Second World Wars, at one point being a field hospital (*see* 'The Forest at War'). Take a right as soon as you hit upon the forest away through the car park and continue down the tarmac path until it starts to curve. Instead of following the path all the way, you can take the path to the left. Both paths lead to the same place but this cuts through a nice bit of woodland. In the evening you will often hear owls hooting. Keep following the path, cross a bridge, taking a moment to enjoy the water flowing underneath, until you come back to a road – take a right and directly in front of you you will see open heathland. This is Ober Heath and, with a little bit of luck, you will be able to see a herd of red deer. You can take the path going through the heath to get a little closer to the deer, but you need to avoid spooking them and moving them on. The ground here is often wet, so stick to the path and keep an eye on where you tread. During early spring you will often see a lapwing flying overhead, making its distinctive pee-wit noise – if he starts to make dives in your general direction it is because you are starting to get a little close to the eggs, which will be in a nest on open heath.

If you are going to be staying until sunset it is worth having a torch on you – open heath can get very boggy, and a torch will make you clearly visible to cars as you walk back. A lot of the roads do not have street lighting and in a lot of cases there are not pavements.

Beaulieu

Beaulieu is a nice town of its own right, and of course it has Beaulieu Abbey and the Motor Museum, though it is not that easy to reach by rail – the nearest station, Beaulieu Road, is three and a half miles away (about an hour's walk) and the trains are very infrequent, except, bizarrely, on a Sunday when they run hourly for most of the day. If you want to do the walk take a right out of the station, taking a second or two to look at the Beaulieu Road Stables, the place where New Forest Pony sales take place at several times throughout the year. The walk is all across open heathland, and it can often be surprisingly cold and windy. However, it is by no means an unpleasant walk, especially if you have the warm sun beating down on you.

Once in Beaulieu you can take the path by the hotel or one a few houses up on the road with the shops. Either way, the path will be marked with signs telling you it is a walk to Buckler's Hard. It is about two miles and is an easy and pleasant walk – though boots are still recommended especially in the spring or after rain as parts can get a little muddy. The walk takes you along the river and plenty of small birds as well as a few swans and ducks can be spotted. About two thirds of the way along you will be presented with a choice of paths, both of which lead to Buckler's Hard. One will cut through the trees and be signposted direct route, however the left fork, although slightly longer, is a much nicer route, taking you much closer to the river. Just before Buckler's Hard there is a bird hide on your left, it is signed and well worth a visit – you might be lucky or you might need a little patience. At the end of it, if it takes your fancy you can look around Buckler's Hard. You will, however, have to walk back the two miles to Beaulieu!

❧ PLACES TO VISIT ❧

Historical places

Rufus Stone – This is the stone marking the supposed spot of the death of King William Rufus in 1100. It is near Stony Cross and there is the aptly named Sir Walter Tyrrell pub nearby (*see* 'Death in the Forest').

Buckler's Hard – Still used as a busy dock, there are always lots of boats present. It boasts a pub and a maritime museum and has plenty of nice walks in the surrounding area. It was used to build ships for Nelson to fight the Spanish Armada, as well as being involved in the D-Day invasion (*see* 'The Forest at War').

Beaulieu – This is by far the most popular and visited attraction within the New Forest, as there is so much to do in one small place. The village itself is a small settlement located on the South Eastern edge of the Forest – but the actual Beaulieu Estate covers a vast 9,000 acres. It is a small village with shops appropriate to the feel of the town – but people generally visit to see the National Motor Museum, Palace House and Beaulieu Abbey. The three attractions, all on the Estate, are covered by one entry fee, though you will need a full day to get the most of it.

The National Motor Museum, originally opened in 1952 as the Montagu Motor Museum, was founded by the 3rd Baron Montagu of Beaulieu in honour of his father, who had been a pioneer of motoring in Britain. Today the museum has grown vastly beyond the original five cars that it held in 1952. By 1972 there were over 300 exhibits and a new building was constructed and the current name adopted. Today there are over 250 cars, including rare early cars and four world land speed record holders. There are also famous cars such as those featured in the *James Bond* films and the Robin Reliant from *Only Fools and Horses*. A more recent attraction are the custom-made cars from the *Top Gear* show. The museum also holds an extensive collection of books, journals, and anything motor related.

Palace House, the second of the large attractions in Beaulieu, was originally the gatehouse to the abbey. It was built in 1204 and was bought by the Montagu family in 1538 following the Dissolution of the Monasteries by Henry VIII. Much extension work was undertaken in the sixteenth and nineteenth centuries, making the Palace House a fine example of a Gothic country house. The house is still the home of the Montagu family but parts of it are open to the public where there is much family history and memorabilia to observe.

The abbey also dates back to 1204 and it too has an interesting history. Unlike Palace House, it suffered a little more and is in semi ruin. It was originally home to Cistercian monks. It is well worth a walk around and, seeing as it is considered one of Britain's most haunted places, you may just bump into a ghost or two (*see* 'Ghostly Goings On').

There are also the lovely gardens for a peaceful stroll and the Secret Army Exhibition, detailing Beaulieu's role in training Churchill's Secret Army (*see* 'The Forest at War').

For information on all of these, including the latest exhibitions and special events, visit www.beaulieu.co.uk.

Calshot – An ancient settlement, dating back to at least the fifth century AD, it has a rich history and fair few things to do. In 1539 Calshot Castle was constructed under the orders of King Henry VIII as part of Britain's coastal defences. It was built using stone from the nearby Beaulieu Abbey. You can now visit the castle, which is owned by English Heritage. There has also been an RAF base on site which has played its part in both world wars (*see* 'The Forest at War'). A little known fact about the town is that the entire population of the Tristan da Cunha Islands was evacuated to Calshot following the 1961 volcanic eruption. The islands are the most remote inhabited archipelago in the word, which in the south Atlantic Ocean are 1,750 miles from the nearest land. The evacuees were moved into former RAF accommodation. Most later returned home but some have stayed on, forming a small community focused around the aptly named road, Tristan Close. To give an idea of the number of people involved the 2009 population figures show total inhabitants of 275 people on the islands.

Hurst Castle – At the southern most point of the New Forest you will find another one of Henry VIII's Device Forts. Just like Calshot Castle, it was built to defend the English coastline from invasion. During its long history it served as a prison for Charles I and played a role during both world wars. The castle is now owned by English Heritage and houses a museum which includes a range of the guns which have been used throughout its history to defend our shores. These range from the 38 ton guns used by the Victorians to the more modern guns of the Second World War. It is also a nice area for a walk. It can be reached by a walk along the spit its situated on or by a frequent ferry from Keyhaven. It offers great views of the Isle of Wight and the Needles.

Wildlife areas

The New Forest Wildlife Park – A wildlife park with an interesting mix of animals, including a few types of otter, both those that you can find in England and those from abroad. Watch out for the Asian Otter lying on its back and playing with stones, whilst the Eurasian Otter is known for its screeching, whining noise. There is a special viewing area for foxes, complete with a one-way window and if you are lucky they will come right up close. There is a selection of owls and some very friendly deer which will inspect you for food. There are also warthogs (February and March are a good time to view the babies, which are surprisingly cute), wolves and lynxes, Scottish wild cats and wallabies just to name a few. There is also a café for food and drink. Close by is Longdown Dairy Farm if you want to visit another nearby attraction (see the section on miscellaneous activities for more information).

Knightwood Oak – The most famous tree in the forest, and the largest oak. A nice area for a picnic, close to Bolderwood Deer Sanctuary. There is a car park a few minutes' walk from the tree (*see* 'Tales of Trees and Other Plants').

Bolderwood Deer Sanctuary – Located at the end of Bolderwood Drive, it is an excellent place to see fallow deer. They are fed at 2 p.m. most days and the deer come pretty close. Do not enter the enclosure though.

Ober Heath – Not far from Brockenhurst, with a car park nearby, it is one of the best places to get a glimpse of red deer as they are often seen grazing here during the last few hours of daylight. However, do not expect to get that close to them, as they tend to be spooked easily. It is reachable from Brockenhurst station although you should allow an hour for the walk if you plan to do this (*see* 'A Few Walks').

New Forest Reptile Centre – All of the UK's native reptiles are kept here in specially designed open-air pens, giving you a good chance of seeing them on a sunny day. The centre plays an important role in conservation, having taken part in several breed and release programmes. It is best visited on a sunny day, when many of the animals can be seen out basking in the sun. Open 10 a.m.–4.30 p.m. April–September. Also here is the RSPB nest cam, showing live footage of a goshawk nest.

Miscellaneous Activities

The New Forest Museum and Visitors' Centre – This is good place to start for an introduction to the Forest and its history and a fun one for children. There is a library attached (which is free to enter) which has a lot of literature on the forest.

Rhinefield House – A stately-home-looking hotel with lovely gardens that serves afternoon tea. Afternoon Tea costs around £13, whilst it is £3.50 for a cup of tea and a plate of free biscuits. If you have the money it is also a nice place to stay the night – if you are covered in mud from your explorations though you may feel a little under dressed!

The Snakecatcher – A pub in Brockenhurst named after the famous Harry 'Brusher' Mills, who spent a large portion of his life as a snake catcher in the New Forest. His favourite pub was later renamed the Snakecatcher in his honour (*see* 'The Snake Catcher'). At the time of writing the pub was being refurbished.

Longdown Dairy Farm – This is a working dairy farm with plenty of hands-on activities for young children, so a great place for families. A farm shop on site sells good produce. It is located near to the New Forest Wildlife Park.

Calshot Activities Centre – Located in Calshot, it is situated in one of the old RAF hangers. If the fancy takes you, you can go rock climbing, dry-slope skiing, or try your hand at a range of water sports. Certainly a good place to visit if you fancy trying something new! See www.calshot.co.uk for more information.

Amews Falconry – Ever fancied learning Falconry? Amews Falconry offer a variety of different courses from a half-day introduction course at £50 up to long term, fully accredited ones. They take place at The Out of Town Centre, in Beaulieu. In the half-day course you will get to handle a bird and learn about their feeding, training and care. Advanced booking is essential; see www.amews.com for more information.

Gardens

Exbury Gardens – These peaceful gardens are located on the edge of the Beaulieu river, a few miles from Beaulieu itself, just across the river from Buckler's Hard. They are well kept with lots to see, including a miniature railway. At the time of writing entry is £8.50 for adults. The site covers 200 acres of woodland garden and is considered one of the finest of its kind in Britain. The Exbury estate was purchased by Lionel Nathan de Rothschild in 1919, soon after the war and he went about creating the gardens that you see today – it was a large undertaking which included three concrete-lined ponds and twenty-two miles of underground piping. During the summer the New Forest Tour open top bus runs to the garden. The miniature steam railway is very popular and proved a huge success after being completed in 2001, the twenty-minute ride, gives you a good view of the gardens and the different plants on show.

Furzey Gardens – Although a good deal smaller than Exbury Gardens, at just 8 acres, it is still worth a visit. Planted in 1922, it is home to numerous rare plants from both the UK and around the world. On site there is also a crafts gallery, café, and a fine art gallery exhibiting work from professional and amateur artists alike. Another interesting building in the gardens is the sixteenth-century Cobb Cottage, a restored building from the 1560s. The cottage is actually built using the timbers from ships and the floorboards are made from wood that was previously used as decking. In the gardens the buildings are roofed with around 1,000 square meters of thatch, and it is a great place to learn a little more about this old and skilled art. There are also play areas for children making this a good half-day visit if you want to explore everything at a relaxed, casual pace.

Travel

The New Forest Tour is an open-top bus that does a two-hour tour of the Forest. It is a great way to explore the National Park, allowing you to get on and off the bus as many times as you like, there is even room for up to four bicycles on the bus, which passes several good cycle routes, allowing you to plan a trip to suit your needs. Included with your ticket you will be given a guide to the New Forest, including some money-off vouchers. The tour runs every hour visiting Lyndhurst, Brockenhurst, Beaulieu, and Exbury Gardens, as well as some campsites along the way. It runs every day in the summer, usually from mid-June to mid-September. For more information on times, dates and prices visit www.thenewforesttour. info. It is around £9 for an all-day adult ticket, but there are large discounts for groups travelling together.

The route was set up in 2004 and is run by Bluestar in partnership with Hampshire City Council, New Forest District

Council and the New Forest National Park Authority. Subsidies were provided for several years in the hope the tour would help to reduce traffic in the New Forest – something that would greatly help the National Park.

The New Forest Show

One of the biggest annual events is the New Forest Show. Lasting three days, it is an eclectic mix of events, shows and stalls. It occurs every year in July, costing around £13 for a ticket.

It is an agricultural show and as such the events are focussed around all things farming, with a good New Forest tint to them. Events common to every year include parades of animals, show jumping, falconry displays, livestock shows and areas for children. The 2010 main event was the Devil's Horseman, a group of stunt riders performing tricks to delight the crowds.

As well as the displays, each year sees a host of stalls taking up the area in New Park, Brockenhurst, where the show is now put on. There are marquees displaying, teaching and selling the following; crafts, antiques, a food fayre (complete with ye old world spelling), arts, blacksmiths and old-time farming just to name a few. It is a popular annual event that draws a crowd of almost 100,000 people each year, generating important revenue for the area, whilst allowing the agricultural industry to show off its finest.

During the show a shuttle bus service is run from Brockenhurst station.

The show itself dates back to 1921, when the New Forest Agricultural and Horticultural Association held a one-day event in August. The show was held at Bartley Cross until 1924 where cattle, pigs, goats, poultry and vegetables were all judged. Parades took place during the afternoon whilst the day ended with music and dancing. It is thought the first ever show drew in around 1,500 people at a cost of 2s 4d a ticket – the show made £404 and gave away £127 in prizes.

Over the next ninety years the location moved around the Forest, with the New Forest Show being held in Lyndhurst, Hinton Admiral and Totton, not settling to its New Park location in Brockenhurst until 1955, where it has been held ever since. In fact, with the exception of during the Second World War, the show has run every year since 1921.

The show has not, however, always been successful in terms of monetary gain. Like so many things in England, it is at the mercy of the weather. Costing around £1 million to put on, three

The Forest is full of adventures around every corner!

successive days of bad weather can really hit them hard. In 2007, after an initially sunny day, the rest of the show was dogged by torrential rain, causing £70,000 to be spent on tractors to tow stranded vehicles and for bark and stone to make the muddy ground usable. Despite this, 68,500 people still attended, but it resulted an overall loss of £200,000 (although this was much better than the £650,000 loss that would have resulted from a cancellation).

Such bad weather, though, is a rarity, so why not go and take a look at a show that will give you an interesting insight into the New Forest and Hampshire from a perspective that is otherwise easy to miss. For more information visit www.newforestshow.co.uk.

🌸 PHOTOGRAPHY 🌸

There is something about taking a picture that appeals to most people, whether it is the act of taking the photo or capturing the memory, it is a pastime that the majority of people take part in at some time or other. But most people will say, particularly concerning wildlife, that they would like to take better photographs.

There are numerous factors that affect the quality of a picture, some that are under you control and some that are not. This section looks at the areas you can control and hopefully will allow you to get a little more out of your camera.

Equipment

First and foremost you will need a camera. If you already have one make sure you are familiar with it. Generally you would have been taking shots in automatic mode. This is where the camera will do everything, apart for zoom, for you. However, most modern digital cameras should allow you to control the exposure and aperture settings. Have a play with your camera, read the manual if necessary and hopefully you can find out how to gain more control over taking your pictures.

Ideally you would want to use an SLR. This stands for Single Lens Reflex. You look through the eyepiece and see directly through the lens (thanks to a prism and a mirror), when you press the button the mirror pops up, exposing either the film or the sensor in the case of digital. It is the mirror going up and down that causes the classic 'click–click' noise associated with cameras, not the shutter, as is generally thought. It gives you the most control over taking the picture and the lenses will give you the best optical quality.

If you are buying a camera there are a few things to consider. Price, of course, is one of them. You can get a perfectly adequate digital compact for less than £100, but if you want an SLR then they are a lot more, you can pretty much spend as much as you want. A high end camera body alone, without any lenses, could cost as much as £6,000, but an entry level SLR can be bought for around £300.

Compacts – Small cameras, compact and lightweight are ideal for travelling and are good for taking quick pictures, but can still give you good quality if you are willing to invest a bit more money. Look for something which gives a decent optical zoom (minimum of 3x if you want to do wildlife shots). Battery life and memory are not as important as they used to be as both have improved significantly in the last five years.

Hybrids – these are slightly larger but are still well suited to travelling. They are, as the name suggests, half way between a compact and an SLR. They will give you better pictures and generally have better lenses. There will also be a more natural way to control exposure and aperture than on a compact. They cannot be fitted in your pocket though.

SLRs – These are the best choice, but by far the most expensive. They allow you full and natural control of everything. Zoom and focus can be done on the lens, whilst there is usually some quick and natural system for getting the exposure and depth of field right (see below). The main strength of the SLR is that you can change lenses depending on what you are after. However, this also means that they will take up a lot more room and weight, not to mention being much more expensive. Choosing an SLR can seem quite daunting, there are a few good makes out there and then you have to buy some lenses on top of it. Generally invest more in the lens than the camera – if you are buying one now it will be digital and the cameras change at a far faster rate than the lenses. Most new ones will also come with self-cleaning sensors. This is where dust is automatically removed from the sensor every time the camera is turned on, something I would have loved to have had on my camera a few years ago! If your friends already have SLRs a good consideration is what brand of camera they have, as you will be able to share lenses if you get the same make of camera (Canon lenses will only fit Canon cameras etc).

Lenses – If you are buying or have an SLR the next consideration is what lenses you will buy or use. Lenses are expensive, often far more than the cameras themselves. They can cost in excess of £6,000 although you do not have to spend nearly that much. One of the most important considerations is what you will be taking photos of. For the purpose of this book we are assuming you will be taking nature shots – to simplify things lenses can be dived roughly into three categories.

- Landscape and scenery – For this you will want a wide-angle lens, meaning you get a large field of vision. Something around a 28-35mm would be well suited, but even with this you will sometimes find you want something a little wider.

- Close ups – If you are taking pictures of small things such as insects, or close up shots of flowers, a macro lens cannot be beaten. It allows you to get very close to a subject. If you get a macro lens you will also benefit from a ring flash – this is a flash that sits in front of the lens and illuminates the subject. This allows you to have a large depth of field while still allowing light in.

- Distance shots – If you want to take pictures of birds, or any animal you cannot get too close to then a telephoto lens is essential. These have a large zoom but are often expensive and heavy. Really you want something that is a minimum of 300mm. If you can afford it then get something with Image Stabilisation (Canon's name for it) or Vibration Reduction (Nikon's name) – this utilises a clever system of counter weights to counteract the effects of lens shake. This means you can hand hold the lens more effectively, and, if there is enough light, maybe do away with the need for a tripod.

To give you an idea of an SLR lens set up, I use three lenses. A 28-85mm lens for everyday shooting and landscapes, it is not ideal for what I want to do but I invested more in my other lenses. I have a 100mm macro with a ring flash for close up shots, and I have a 100-400mm telephoto lens with Images Stabilisation. I run this off a 1.4x converter, which makes it a 140-560mm. This gives the advantage of making it suitable to more situations than a fixed focal length (also known as a primary lens). Sadly, including the camera and everything else, this weights well over 5kg, not ideal for travelling light!

Tripods – whether or not you take one of these will depend on a few things: how much you want to carry, what lens you use, if you will be staying mostly in one place and what light levels/exposure you want. The general rule of thumb is the darker/less light you are letting in, and the higher the zoom you are using the more likely you are to need a tripod. Have a play with your camera, taking a few shots, and see how much you benefit from having a tripod. Generally, though, you will always benefit from having a tripod but how you stand and using natural objects can greatly help to reduce camera shake (caused by your arms moving by tiny amounts). Sometimes a tripod is not practical to use, or convenient to take with you.

The basics

So now that you have your camera and maybe some lenses it is time to take some pictures. The first thing you need is a subject; choose something easy to start with – in the New Forest one of the New Forest Ponies would be ideal. They are big, they will not be scared off and they will, unlike most animals, usually stay still for you.

Before you take your shot there are a two things you need to know about, these are aperture and exposure. This is not a book on how to take photographs so it will be brief and to the point – if you want more detail there are hundreds of good books on the subject.

Aperture – This is the measure of how much of the lens remains open to let light in. The wider the aperture (the lower the f-number) the more light is let in, but the lower the depth of field. This means that less of the image is in focus. A low depth of field can be great if you want just the subject in focus with the background being soft and blurry. If you have a small aperture you have less light, but much more of the image in focus. The closer you are to something the larger the depth of field you will need and the higher the f-stop – this is almost always the case with macro photography. This means that the aperture, the actual opening allowing light in, is very small. This means that there will not be enough light from natural sources so a ring flash is often needed.

Exposure time – This determines how long the light falls on the sensor or on the film. There are two things to consider with this. Firstly it is getting the right exposure – you do not want it too light or too dark. Your camera will tell you what the exposure is like, and with a digital camera you can always take a shot and have a look at it. Play with the settings to see how it changes. The other thing to consider is motion – at its simplest, the lower the exposure the less movement will be captured. If you have a bird flapping its wings a low exposure time, of around 1/250th of a second, will take a snap shot of the creature giving the impression of time being frozen, with its wings still in the air. If you take it with a longer exposure (around 1/10th of a second) its wings will be blurred as in the time you took your picture the wings would have moved. Experiment and see what you like, part of the art of photography is about capturing motion on a still image. Be careful though as the longer the exposure, the more likely it is that the image will be blurred from camera shake as well as having the lighter (such as the white) areas of the image overexposed.

Taking the photograph

How to stand – Find something that is comfortable for you, while trying to keep the camera as still as possible. If you have a tripod fantastic, or you can use a wall, stone or branch to steady the camera. If you have a large lens it can help to hold your elbow to your body giving good support for the lens.

Composure – Think about where you want the animal and what else you would like in the picture. Generally avoid having everything central, a photograph is usually better if your eye is drawn away from the centre to look at something. A quick rule of thumb that is often used is the 'rule of thirds'. If you imagine a picture divided up into nine equal squares (like a noughts and crosses game), then important compositional elements (such as the subject and the horizon) should appear on these lines or where they cross.

If you can, be at the eye level of the animal, it gives a much more natural feel to the photo than if you are looking down or up, though of course with birds in trees this is not always an option! Remember, however, that it is a personal choice, and you have to take photographs that you are happy with and everyone has their own tastes.

Lighting – As mentioned above, you need to decide on the depth of field (using the f-number) and the exposure time to get the right amount of light and the right amount of the picture in or out of focussed as desired. Usually it is best to have the sun behind you as shadows in front of the animal often appear odd, though this is not always the case. The richest light for photography is usually the couple of hours before dusk and after dawn, even if the latter is not the most sociable time of day! Think about where the shadows are going to fall, often a shadow can give the picture some depth, whereas if it is in midday sun the image can look flat and lifeless – the best way is to play around, take different photos under different conditions and see what works.

Format – If your camera allows it, take the picture in RAW format. This means that it is not converted by the camera into jpg. When you convert to a format certain information is thrown away – you want to do this as late as possible. RAW gives you the highest quality and the most options for editing if you want to do this later.

Photoshop – How much or little you use Photoshop is entirely a personal choice. If you know what you are doing it can do everything you could do in a darkroom and a whole lot more. You can correct exposures, colours, choosing to highlight certain areas and remove unwanted blemishes (be it dust or a branch of a tree.) I do not use Photoshop to alter away from the natural appearance of the image; all the photos in this book had no more than a few seconds of going through Photoshop – mostly to remove the blemishes and marks that have resulted from dust on the lens and sensor.

The best thing though is just to go out and take photos, learn by doing and find your own style. Remember that photography should be fun!

🌿 FIELD CRAFT AND STALKING 🌿

Getting close to an animal, and getting those good sightings or shots is an art in itself. Of course it dates back thousands of years, long before the camera or the term wildlife enthusiast had ever been invented. The techniques used all have their basis in hunting, with everything but the end game being the same. In a hunt, to make the kill, you would often need to get as close as possible, especially before the development of ranged weapons and traps. If the animal knew you were there then it would more often than not be too late. With photography the goal is the same, except instead of killing an animal you want to get that elusive picture.

Know what you are after

Do you want to catch a glimpse or get a perfect shot? Depending on your goals you will use drastically different methodologies. While approaching animals may well utilise the same techniques, your aims will affect other considerations. If you are just after a sighting, with an attempt at identifying the creature, considerations such as the position of the sun, your elevation level and light levels are not so important. If you want that perfect shot, your position relative to theirs is much more key. Decide what you want before you go out and you will be far more likely to get what you are after.

A big consideration is how far you are willing to go and how serious you want to be, some people will go in full camouflage, camped out in one spot for days, making sure they smell of the forest, not having eaten anything which will give them a scent, they will rub dirt and mud into their face. Others will just be quieter when they think they are getting close.

Know your subject

Depending on what animal you are after will change how you behave. Firstly there are the obvious things, such as habitat. If you are looking for a certain type of fish there's no point going to heathland. Look at the type of area the animal likes to live in, what its habits are and from this you will be able to narrow down your area of search. Time of day can be extremely important, red deer are generally better to spot at dawn and dusk, when they settle down to graze, whereas lizards and snakes can often be easier to spot in the midday sun, when they can come out to bask. If you are after birds of prey then think about what they hunt and therefore where they are likely to be.

Find out a bit about their behaviour, strengths and weaknesses. Do they rely more on sight or smell? Birds tend to have excellent sight and hearing, but poor sense of smell, whereas deer will spot you more by smell and noise, detecting you with these senses far sooner than they will see you.

Finally look out for tell-tale marks of the animal, mostly these will be in the form of tracks and droppings – fresh tracks and fresh droppings means you might not be that far away.

Dress sensibly

You should wear clothes that fulfil a couple of criteria. Firstly they should be of appropriate colours, as natural to where you will be as possible. Earthy, woody colours for a forest are best. The aim is to break up your outline, making you less noticeable and certainly less human. The other consideration is that you want your clothes to be quiet. Avoid anything that rustles when you walk, or is so loose that it is going to catch on branches around you. Shoes are important … it is a balance between keeping your feet clean and dry, being stable on your feet and being able to feel where you put you feet.

Keep an eye out

It goes without saying that you need to be observant at all times. In day-to-day life you tend to focus on one object, only relying on your peripheral vision for large, startling movements. And this is how your eyes work – you use the centre of your retina to detect detail and colour, whereas the outside of your vision is intended to detect motion, namely threats. So it is normal for you, as you walk around, to focus on one thing. You need to get more used to relying on your peripheral vision, constantly rescan the area around you, each time focussing on different objects, not just one point in front of you. If you just look at one point you will tend to focus on that, each time taking in less and less of your surroundings, change what you look at, look where you normally would not, between branches, around trees, not just where you are going and where you are treading. Finally, if you spot what you are looking for, do not take your eyes off it. If the animal moves off, or the bird is flying, it can be extremely hard to see where it is going unless you have your eyes firmly fixed on it.

Walk quietly and stay hidden

It goes without saying that you need to be walking as quietly as possible and there are special techniques to help you go unnoticed.

Position is important ... try not to outline yourself against the sun; you will be visible to anything and everything. Try and stay downwind if you can, not only will this hide your scent from the animals, but it will also help to hide your noise a little as well.

How you choose to walk again depends on how serious you want to take things. Obviously as you go along you want to make as little noise as possible, that means not walking on crackling leaves or branches and twigs which will snap loudly underfoot. The easy thing that everyone can do is to plan ahead, look at the route you are going to take before you get there – this will also help you avoid boggy and marshy areas you are going to sink in. Avoid, if you can, constantly staring at where you are going to place your feet, whilst this will make you more stable and quieter, you are unlikely to spot anything at all.

If your shoes are light enough you can employ a certain type of walking. Normally people put down there heel first, then roll it over to the ball, an efficient and stable way of walking, but not one designed for stealth. Instead keep the weight on your back foot, and place the forward foot down on its side, rolling it over slowly, only putting it down if there is no resistance, lifting it if you feel a stick underfoot. Of course if you are in thick soled walking boots then you would not necessarily feel this – it is for this reason that some people even go bare foot!

The approach

Once you have spotted an animal it is important to approach them slowly. Not only do you want the creature to stay where they are, but you do not want to startle them – scaring them off can do a lot more harm than you realise. Young could be abandoned, or, if it is during the winter when food and energy are scarce, fleeing from you could tip the balance enough to affect the animal's chance of survival. As you walk towards them go as slowly as you can, if the animal looks at you then pause until it takes its attention away from you.

Do not move the animals on; if they start to look uncomfortable then stay where you are. If they do start to move then leave them be and move on to another area. In the case of a herd of deer it is quite simple, if one or two move to the other side of the herd, you are as close as you are going to get; if you try and get any closer the whole herd is likely to move on. Not only is this unfair to the animals that are most likely trying to feed, but it is also breaking local bylaws. If you move them on from their local feeding ground you are more likely to push them towards car parks and roads where they will be at risk of being hit by cars.

If you want to be really serious …

This bit is purely for information, and it is something that very few people will ever do, but the techniques may be interesting to some.

Descenting – Some animals have an amazingly good sense of smell. A dog's, for example, is thousands of times better than ours. For this reason, if you want to take things seriously, how you smell is very important – it is one more thing that you need to hide from the animals that you are trying to spot. This process of getting rid of your smell, known as descenting, starts days before you even get anywhere near your target. What you smell like comes down to a few things, what you eat, how much you sweat, and what you wash with. Those taking this seriously will not eat any strong smelling foods for a few days, this means any garlicky food is out. On the day even things like chocolate or salt and vinegar crisps will give you away. Only wash with natural soaps, nothing fragranced, that goes for deodorants too. Any smell that does not belong in a forest will seem unnatural to the animals and will alert them to your presence. You can go one step further, and go to saunas to make yourself sweat out your smell, cleaning your pores and then adopting the smell of the forest, using forest leaves to gain its scent. Of course these are quite large lengths and by no means necessary to catch a glimpse of an animal!

Hides and camouflage – some photographers even spend a period of time living in locations that they think the animals they are after are going to frequent. If you are in one place for a long time and are well hidden the animals will get more used to your presence as they

realise that you are not a threat. This can be utilised over a shorter period. If you choose a location where you think you might spot deer, and wait there, quietly, without moving, the deer will be more likely to come close to you. If you are making a small 'hide' make sure to use natural materials, branches and leaves from the location you are waiting in. Camouflage works by breaking up your outline, making you much harder to spot, often photographers will wear specially designed camouflage clothes similar if not identical to the ones used by soldiers in the army – the aim after all is the same, to not be spotted.

Enjoy yourself

At the end of the day, you should be enjoying what you do, enjoying nature and the New Forest – you can take things as seriously or as lightly as you want when you are looking for animals. It is true that being more relaxed about your attitude and being a little noisier may result in fewer sightings, but if you will have fun while doing it does it really matter? Some of my most successful days in terms of photography have been my least enjoyable, as it has meant sitting in one, rather cold place all day, waiting for that one shot – on the other hand, some of my most enjoyable have been a relaxed stroll with a chance encounter. Just remember, respect the New Forest, respect the animals you are trying to see and have fun while you do it.

Other titles published by The History Press

The New Forest at War
JOHN LEETE

The New Forest at War documents aspects of the social and military history of this unique area of Britain during the years of the Second World War. The area was on the front line of the massive build-up and launch of D-Day in June 1944. It is well illustrated with photographs, maps and documents, and contains many first-hand accounts of life in the New Forest during the war. It will be of great interest to everyone who lives and works in the Forest, to visitors and all those with an interest in Britain's wartime heritage.

978 0 7524 5193 0

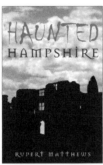

Haunted Hampshire
RUPERT MATTHEWS

This well-researched book showcases almost 100 ghostly encounters from around Hampshire. Here you will discover ghostly seamen haunting the King's Bastion at Portsmouth, spirits of the Roundheads galloping through Crondall and a haunted megalith at Mottistone. Exploring everything from pubs and churchyards to castles and ports, *Haunted Hampshire* will appeal to anyone interested in the supernatural history of the area.

978 0 7524 4862 6

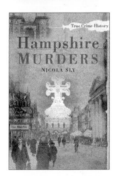

Hampshire Murders
NICOLA SLY

Life in the historic county of Hampshire has not always been peaceful, for over the years it has experienced numerous murders. These include the killing of 'Sweet Fanny Adams' in 1867; the horrific murder committed by the postmaster at Grayshott in 1901; and the gun battle in the village of Kingsclere in 1944, which resulted in the deaths of three people. Nicola Sly's carefully researched, well-illustrated and enthralling text will appeal to anyone interested in the shady side of Hampshire's history.

978 0 7509 5106 7

Hunting in Britain From the Ice Age to the Present
BARRY LEWIS

Exploring sites such as Creswell Crags, Chatsworth House, Stafford Castle, Cheddar Gorge and the New Forest, *Hunting in Britain* examines the role of hunting through time and considers how it shaped the landscape as we know it. Bringing together for the first time evidence from the Palaeolithic to the modern era, and studying both the archaeology and history of hunting, this book provides a fresh understanding of man's complex relationship with the natural world.

978 0 7524 4802 2

Visit our website and discover thousands of other History Press books.

www.thehistorypress.co.uk